HOOVES HARNESS HARDWORK

Ploughmen of Yesteryear

by **Ernest Taylor**

D0318748

Finavon Print & Design

First published in Great Britain in 1997 by
Finavon Print & Design
3 Cadgers Path, Finavon,
Angus. Scotland. DD8 3QB

Reprinted 1998

Typesetting & printing by Finavon Print & Design

Cover: Laura Christie

Illustrations: Ron Forbes

ISBN 0-9528813-2-2

© The Wee Book Press, 68 Millgate, Friockheim, Angus. DD11 4TN

All rights reserved. No part of this publication may be reproduced, stored in a retrieval system, or transmitted, in any form or by any means, electronic, mechanical, photocopying, recording or otherwise, without the prior permission of the Copyright owner.

Contents

Introduction   5

Foot Prints in the Snow   8

To the Ploughman of yesteryear   10

The Cottar Man   12

By a ploughman of many yesteryears   14

The Back Breaker   16

Germ Free   22

The Bachelor Ploughman or The Bothy Lad   24

The Maid Threw Down The Towel   29

One Life Gone Eight to Go   30

The Horse, His Feed, His Shelter   32

Mistaken Identity   34

The Day The Thrashing Mill Cam In Aboot   38

Harvesting the Hay   42

The Cottar Kids   45

The Pig Killing   57

The Only Time They Left The Land   59

The Farmer Nailed the Apprentice   61

Sixteen Years with no Remission   62

Twelve and a Tanner a Bottle   64

The Birds and the Bees   64

The Farmer and the Fire Brigade   67

To Be a Farmers Boy   68

Oor Auld Porridge Pot   69

Memories   70

Hot Feet   71

The Tail of a Stable Rat   73

The Horseman's Word   74

Reduction in farm servants wages   78

The Auld Crafters Roup   83

The Clydesdale   86

Great Days of the Heavy Horse   87

Finally   99

In this book there are a number of old photographs of the ploughmen of yesteryear with their Clydesdale working companions. Perhaps some of the readers may be able to identify the men and locations shown in the photographs.

Introduction

I have decided to write this book because of my admiration for these men who were a breed unto themselves. Not only were they great horsemen, but clever in all aspects of their work. No radio or television, thus they had time on their hands which they used to the full.

For instance, if their horse's harness needed cleaning, it would be brought from the stable to the bothy. In many cases they would give it a good grounding. This was done by using a tool called a Beattle - a piece of hardwood shaped at one end like a wedge, which was rubbed very hard on to the leather, so that when polished, the leather would have a nice geeter (polish). This was what they called their tricking harness. In other words, the harness for travelling away from the farm - possibly into town for materials such as coal, grass seed, or whatever.

In those days, they took a great pride in competing with other farm outfits, always making sure theirs was, in their opinion, the best. Farm traffic was by horse and cart, to the railway station and elsewhere, this being their main means of transportation.

It was said necessity was the mother of invention. That being so, I'm sure many good ideas were produced by these hard-working men, and in many cases they had to be inventive to find an easier way of doing things.

Coming back to the harness, we have men who still carry on this great art of producing show harness. One especially, the late Allan McRae from Forebank, near Brechin, was a master at the craft. All the decorations were of his own making. The polish he used was his own mixture, and when he died, he took with him his secret recipe.

The finished article was a thing of great workmanship and beauty. I remember watching the ploughmen carrying out their chores using polish called Black Beauty, with a horse's head on the tin. The draught-chains, or whatever, were made of steel, and had to be polished. The method was to put the chains and a quantity of bran into a jute sack, tie one end to a fixed object, and proceed to move the sack backwards and forwards - or they would fix the sack to the shakers of the threshing mill, and the shaker arms would do the rest.

Should they be showing a horse and cart, the latter would have to be washed thoroughly, after which the paint was applied. The washing was usually carried out at the burn, as running tap-water was rarely heard of. After all their hard work, they might not be judged a prize winner, but had put in as much hard work as the one judged the best.

The labour that goes into getting the horse up to standard would take many hours of washing, grooming, pleating the main and tail, and also giving great attention to the legs and feet. Quite often, the night before the competition, the ploughman would stay in the stable with his horse, in case, after being brought to perfection, the horse would lie down and undo his good work.

Another champion with a great interest in horse and harness is Bob Cameron, The Muirdrum.

The ploughman usually was very kind, proud and very good to his horses, and looked after them as if they were his own children. On a cold winter's night he would return to the stable and give his pair a nice sweet swede neep, or a bran and treacle mash. This was the same bran as we have today for breakfast. The farms used to keep a barrel of treacle for the livestock in general.

There was something nice about going into a stable on a cold winter's night. When the door was opened, like music to your ears, that welcome nicher, as much as to say, "We appreciate you paying us a visit, just hope you've got a titbit with you." The heat generated by these massive hulks of bone and muscle made the stable feel as if it was centrally heated.

Men and their horses - two breeds of the past - not forgetting the wives and families who knew little else but meagre rations and hard work.

Nostalgia has played a big part in the writing of these tales of the past. Sixty-five years ago I was laddie, 11 years old. My main road was to the farm. It was a great thrill to be in the company of these men and their Clydesdales. Even at that age it was something special to look at the art of ploughing a straight furrow, or drilling for potatoes, or whatever.

6

Another hard job was the emptying of the cattle courts, where layer after layer of straw, the cattle's winter bedding, had to be removed and put into a midden. This material had now become dung, and being put into a solid heap advanced the rotting process, ready for when it would be scattered on the fields.

In the days of the horse, they had a method that gave even distribution over the field. It was taken from the midden to the field, or sometimes direct from the court. The cart was put on the steep slant, pushed up at the front, fixed at an angle, and the back door removed. The man used a tool called a hak to pull the material out, then it was put into heaps and carefully measured to give even distribution. That was known as dunging on the face of the land, ready for the plough.

Foot Prints in the Snow

The bothy frying pan

The frying pan was needed on very rare occasions, the bothy lads having very little to put in it apart from the eggs recovered from various parts of the farm. They would be found in the straw rick, the hay hake, the cattle court or elsewhere. You name it, the ploughman knew where to look.

The minister arrived to pay his untimed visit just as the lads were about to make their tea. The fire was lit ready for the kettle and the frying pan to be put into position. Looking at the frying pan with staring eyes, the minister noticed the white fat, the remains of the previous sausage fry up, the Sunday treat. He also saw what looked like footmarks in the snow but instead of snow it was white fat where the mice had had a party. The minister then asked the ploughman how he would remove the footmarks. The reply was very simple, "Just place the pan on the fire and they disappear". After the fat had melted he noticed black specks in the pan and remarked, "You've got soot amongst the fat". The reply was, "Na! Na! That's nothing as serious as soot. That's the mouse's calling card! A narrow squeak.

To the Ploughman of yesteryear

I've heard them called the Lantern Ploughmen. You may ask, "Why the name?" In the days when there was no electricity, the main source of lighting for the ploughman was the paraffin lantern, which was also used as a portable light. It was used to light the stable when attending to the horses, and it was also hung up in the bothy.

My grandfather had the tailor's shop in Colliston village, where many of the ploughmen came for their clothes. The usual wardrobe might be as follows:

1 tailor-made blue serge suit for dress, single-breasted.
2 pairs of Long John plaiden drawers.
2 blue flannel shirts with mother of pearl buttons, and three detachable white collars.
1 pair corduroy trousers.
1 pair moleskin trousers.
1 greaser, as today's denim jacket.
1 bonnet with snoot snib.

Many of them would pay but there were always a few who promised to pay later, but later never came. He would move to another farm. With communications very difficult he might never be found.

Bonnets, as caps were known, were quite often adorned with a straw plait made by the ploughman in the shape of a lovers' knot. Another thing was what they called a shaky pheasant, usually won at the "switchies" or fair, possibly on the hoopla or ringboard. They looked like a pheasant and were fixed on a spring clip. This was also in the cap, and when the owner moved his head they would appear to be shaking, hence the name.

Having mentioned the tailor's shop, to see them in action was very interesting. There were what you called tramp tailors, tradesmen who tramped from place to place, mostly at the terms, May and November.

I've seen tailors sitting facing each other on a huge board like a table, raised two feet off the floor. This was called the cutting board and kept the material they were working with from falling on the floor. Each tailor sat cross-legged, one leg under the other. When they finished sewing a suit, they had to iron it into shape. They did this with a board across their knees, a wet cloth, and a 12-pound solid pressing iron, heated in a small stove specially for the job. The wet cloth was placed over the material, the iron was then thumped up and down, pressing the cloth, hence the fact that nearly all tailors were bow-legged.

They mostly smoked what was known as a Stonehaven pipe complete with lid to avoid fire. Once it was lit, it never left their lips. Now, part of the skill was when the juices collected in the mouth, they never swallowed. The art was to spit them out into what was known as a spitoon - a round object made of porcelain, dark brown in colour to match the spit. I've seen three tailors, all smoking pipes and using the spitoons. Out of the sides of their mouths would come the tobacco refuse, without looking it landed bang on target.

This may have been a dirty habit - even so, it was well executed. Many a bomb aimer would have been glad of the art.

The Cottar Man
Married Man

His habits were very simple - dedication and hard work. If he drove a pair of horse like the single man, they were his pride and joy. Their comforts came first, after which he would attend to his own.

They were usually fee'd on contract for one year. You can understand, having a wife and family and to be on the move too often was not desirable. Usually on a big farm, the grieve and the foreman were married men. Their house was tied with the job, which meant, no job, no home. It was quite common for some of the farmers to have words with the worker, when he would tell him, "You're sacked, and you've got 24 hours to get off my land."

That meant vacate the house - furniture, family, livestock - the lot. He would employ another man who would be in the house within 24 hours of the first man receiving his notice.

The Highland Clearances and the cottar man's clearances had the same ring about them, but the Good Lord doesn't pay his debts in money. Quite often, the married men's wives were out-workers, poo'in' neeps, dressing tatties, lousing sheaves at the mill and many other chores. There was also the house to keep, the bairns to feed and clad ready for the school. Two days' work in one.

The houses were often no better than a pigsty. Their floors were flagstones laid on top of black earth, which, if covered with lino, was so damp the lino would rot away in no time. All the housewife could do was wash the stones to keep them clean. The walls, likewise, were plastered on whin bools. That was the building material gathered from the fields to build the houses.

Having said that, quite a number were built with sandstone or whatever, but the hair and lime plaster was definitely applied on to the hard surface. With no damp course, the result was that when the fire was lit, it drew the moisture into the room, causing condensation.

Their only means of heating and cooking, drying wet clothes or getting hot water was usually a black range, which had a very difficult oven to control. In addition, they would dry their kindling or logs in it. Sometimes, at one side of the range would be a small boiler, which held approximately two gallons of water, with a small brass tap to drain it. This had to be filled by hand, usually with the big black kettle that was always available for such chores.

The house consisted of a "but an ben" - that was a kitchen and a large bedroom. The "but" would today be called the living room - the "ben" the large bedroom.

In those days, families were large. There was no bathroom and in most cases no running water, but sometimes a tap or spigot outside, also a very small back kitchen. A dry lavatory (or watery or WC) was usually at the foot of the garden.

Above the fire you would often find a "swee" - that was a large bracket hinged to move over the fire for hanging your kettle, various pots, etc. The arm that came over the fire had four rings, each one with a hook, allowing the various pots to be hung above the fire at the same time.

There were various perks, such as tatties, coals, firewood, oatmeal, milk, and of course, free rent plus probably a wee drop bruised corn for the pigs' boiler, mixed with boiled tatties and mixen (powdered grain) from the miller.

I'm sure I've only touched on the married men and their manners of yester years. What an honour to have known you.

By a ploughman of many yesteryears

This story was given to me by a man of the land many many years ago. He explained he was only 14 years of age working the single horse or orra beaster on the farm and in a bothy with another four older men. They had no entertainment, not even a wireless set which meant they played dominoes or whatever. They didn't even have cycles which meant they were hardly away from the farm, when all the wishful thinking was centred around the farm house maid. In this case it was the farmer's two sons who were courting her. After a considerable time had passed she was being walked out by one of them when he stopped and asked her if he could ask a personal question. She replied, "go ahead, anything you like." Sheepishly he put the question "I would like to know between my brother and me, who makes the best love?." She hesitated then gave her reply, "It's like this. Your father would make six of the two of you."

The Back Breaker

Now is the time for reflection. How often I hear people saying, "Do you remember the two weeks of torture, aided by the Education Board - tattie holidays?" I never understood where the holiday bit came into it. The time has come for the auld togs to be looked oot - a time when your older brothers' cast-offs seemed to be made for you. If you complained about his cut-down coat sleeves being four inches too long, the answer would be "They're meant to be," or, "It's tattie time - that's the fashion." But it was time to draw the line when you saw your sister's skirt produced.

Speaking of old clothes, I had an older brother's coat which had been cut down to suit my size - well, approximately. The reason I mention it is included in a story below.

My mother and father died and left six of a family, both having been in their 30s. As I have said before, there was a lady standing in the wings ready to fill their post. She was my mother's sister, Auntie Maggie, but to me and another five, Mother Maggie. You've heard of the lady with the lamp - she didn't have one, but she still comes into my list of supreme awards.

She never asked us to do anything that she didn't do herself. For instance, we went to the tattie planting, tattie picking, etc. Despite having so much on her hands, getting all sleepy-heads up in the morning - 6.30 for the tattie picking time - she still went with us.

She had very little time in the morning, the pieces (sandwiches, etc.), would be made the night before, and put into the various coat pockets. Remember, we weren't back at the house until possible 5.30 in the evening. This meant four pickers' rations for a full day had to be prepared for four young growing laddies, always hungry.

We would leave the village and walk two miles to the field where you were to be picking - dark when you left in the morning, likewise when you returned.

Back to the coat where the food for the day had been put into the pockets the previous night. En route to the fields I felt something moving in my pocket. Slipping my hand in I found there was something pretty big and fluffy with lots of movement. One of my brothers had a great idea to dispose of whatever was in my pocket. He lifted up a piece of branch from a tree and struck my pocket with great success. Whatever was in there had gone still - the only trouble was he hit me so hard on my hip, I was sore for the rest of the day.

We proceeded with the operation where I removed my coat, turned it upside down, and as I did, not only did my food drop out, but also a large rat whose blood was everywhere. This rendered my sandwiches unfit for human consumption, which meant the rations had to be shared.

In those days, the mornings seemed to be very cold with hard frost. You were chilled to the bone walking to the field, never mind picking tatties, still dark with daylight breaking, - and you could hardly see 50 yards ahead.

Everybody had been given what they called a bit or a half-bit to pick - that was a measured area of the drill. A full bit would measure, depending on the farm, about 32 feet. A bit was just what it said, a bit of the whole drill. The grieve would measure and put in a pin, which was normally a piece of broom cut from the side of the field. When your neighbours weren't looking, to move the pin and lessen the size of your bit used to be the trend, but never a great success.

Usually, the person at the "in ging" regulated the timing, and would speed up when the digging machine came into the drill, when the rest of the pickers would have to start picking.

The in ging is the end or entry to the drill, and that person is usually someone connected with the farm, e.g. farmer's wife or grieve's wife, who usually had this bit with a lot of blanks caused by working the land at the various stages. They were finished before anyone else, speeding the workings up and making it hard for the folk who were picking the full crop.

When the rain started to spitter, it was a great thought that you would be homeward bound very soon, but this seldom happened. It was wet enough to lift your hopes, and at the same time make everybody wet and miserable.

If you were putting the tatties in wicker sculls, they weighed so heavy with soil baked on to them. Picking was bad enough, but what about the ploughman lad who had to lift them on to the cart? Should it be the wire-bottomed boxes with the bow handle, they were much easier to lift.

Quite often, they would have a young lad standing on the shafts of the cart, catching as they were thrown up, and when empty dropping them back on your bit.

To stick the digger was a disgrace, which meant that when the cart arrived at your bit to collect your tatties, you hadn't finished picking and it had to wait for you to do so.

By this time, the digger had to wait as well, and, of course, no sooner did you finish when before your eyes another fresh picking of tatties awaited you.

Robert Burns said toothache was the hell o' a' diseases - all I can say is, he never picked tatties.

Another trick we used to try, if there was a large stone available, was to place it on top of the drill, hoping it would cause the digger if not to stop at least to slow down, but all in vain.

Something that stands out was the ploughman stopping the cart, putting his back to the wheel, gripping the top with his hands, and putting his feet into the spokes at the bottom. Asking his horse to go forward, he went round as the cart moved on, adding weight for extra traction. Quite a dangerous act.

Wild life was often to be seen. Young rabbits would be thrown out by the reel of the digger, amazingly very seldom hurt, or a field mouse would scurry over the newly churned ground. Another wee creature to appear was occasionally the mole, having been disturbed from his underground world.

It was a strange thing, that no matter how sore your back was, when we had finished oor lunch we headed for the barn to play hide and seek, or just romp amongst the straw - and yet, before you stopped, your back was at breaking point.

One thing that got me annoyed was, if you asked the grieve what time it was, he would take his watch from his pocket and, after a delay, reply "Tattie time."

One of the most cruel things I ever witnessed - one morning the potato drills were so hard with frost, the pair of horses in the digger couldn't pull it. But have no fear, help was near, in the form of a farmer who had a bright idea! He got a bunch of straw and placed it under the horses, and set fire to it. The animals took off. After a few yards the digger came out of the drill and so did the horses, galloping into the open ground where the pickers were standing. The machine, travelling at speed, was all over the place. Eventually, the horses were brought to a halt in a state of nerves, and trembling with fear. One of them had to be taken back to the stable, as it was so badly blistered. The farmer concerned was very lucky. Had the people who witnessed the act been in a position to do something about it, I'm sure any treatment handed out to him would have been the same.

The wages paid for one day's work were four shillings and six pence - 4/6. That's twenty-two-and-a-half pence in today's money for a nine-hour day - plus your travelling time to and from the farm. The only difference, in my opinion, from slaves, was, we didn't have ankle clamps and chains. The tatties were loaded on to the carts and taken away to what they called the tattie pit. This was a shallow scoop, dug out of the earth approximately 12 inches deep and nine feet wide, height depending on the amount of potatoes which were tipped into position by the carts. They were built up in the form of a triangle, covered over with a layer of wheat straw a foot deep. Ten inches of soil was dug out to form a trench at either side to act as drainage. The length varied according to the amount of potatoes. This type of housing for the tatties had to be waterproof and frostproof.

Another time-learned art. Every boy received their pay usually a few days after finishing at the respective farm. I can remember sitting in the kitchen waiting for the pay to arrive - just over a pound for five-and-a-half days' work, and ten years off your life - at least, it felt like that. The big thrill was thinking the money was yours, only to discover you were only allowed to handle it. Of course there were other roads for it, meaning new boots, etc., for the school. Every penny had to be accounted for.

I forgot to mention the harrowing. This was when an implement called a harrow, consisting of three iron frames with spikes which, when pulled by the horses, went into the soil and brought to bring to the surface any ungathered potatoes. This operation was carried out by means of all the pickers, who were spread out in a line across the field. With box in hand you picked the loose potatoes. If someone was a dirty bit picker, this is where it was done for them. This was another backbreaker, having to walk with a box containing a lot of tatties, up and down the length of the field.

I was asked by my grandchildren, "When you came back home at night you didn't have a TV or wireless - what did you do?"

The answer was very simple - when you got back, there was a large tin bath waiting, and a washing boiler full of hot water. Remember, every drop had to be drawn from the well - in other words, it was carried in and carried out.

Of course, you dropped your dirty clothes and after your bath put on something fresh. Remember, somebody had to clean and dry the tattie clothes ready for the morning, and that someone was Maggie.

There's one thing that stands out in my mind. As I said, somebody had to get the bath water ready, and the food, etc. She, my auntie, would say to us at the tattie field, "Now, boys, I am going away early to get things ready at the house. You'll have to pick my bit for the last three rounds of the digger."

After she left, we would sometimes have a discussion like, "Who does she think she is, dodging picking the tatties?" In fact, we reckoned it was almost a criminal offence that had been committed!

They say hard work never killed anyone. She lived to be 95 years of age, but by the amount of work she did, 195 would have been just about right. When my grandchildren ask what we did for entertainment, I say, "First your bath, second your food, but the greatest kick was when you crawled into bed to find that pig clay hot water bottle, usually wrapped in a piece of towelling that served two purposes - in case the screw on top of the bottle leaked, and to keep it from burning your feet." I can still feel my weary bones being caressed with the radiated heat, not even remembering to wish myself good night, but, O Boy, was that entertainment or was it?

Of course, come 5.30 a.m., your bones had recovered, but, alas, your eyes were the problem, thinking it was still closing time.

Summing up, a horrible thought the tattie howking, with the word "slavery" rearing its ugly head.

Germ Free

This is a story about the bothy men, their manners and their habits. The ploughman's furniture was very limited, often with no table. Each man had two kists, one for clothes, the other for food which was usually his seat, but was a bad height for cutting on his half loaf of bread. He had a great art when slicing same, and as there were no sliced loaves, they had to be cut by hand. This was executed as if a mechanical slicer had carried out the operation. He put the bread on his knee, spread it with butter or whatever then proceeded to cut it across. On one occasion the Minister was paying a visit and noticed he was cutting the bread resting on his dirty trousers, the same ones he had been wearing when removing the dung from the cattle court. He couldn't resist the chance to if there would be a lot of germs where the bread was resting on his knee. "O aye," he replied, "there are lots of germs, but its a richt if you gi' the last bit a guid scrape."

THE Bachelor Ploughman
or
The Bothy Lad

Now, this is where men were men, and had to be. He, the above mentioned, now came into his own, rough and ready. Well, plenty rough, but nothing ever ready, including his meals. The bothy, a place of pleasant vulgarity - the only difference between the trenches in France and the bothy, there was a roof on it.

First of all to describe it, you have to smell it. A perfume of double strength sweat coming from tacketty boots newly removed from a pair of feet. They were lined with straw to absorb the sweat as they walked many miles in a day. In fact, a man with a pair of horses harrowing would walk 36 miles in a nine-hour day at a speed of four miles per hour. The straw in the boots, you could say was the first odour-eaters that didn't.

Apart from the insides, the boots themselves were impregnated with dung juices from the cattle and their horses. They tell me it was so bad, the bothy cat stayed at the door.

I can remember when the bothy lads got dressed with the blue serge suit, blue flannel shirt with mother-of-pearl buttons and detachable white collar. They all had the same strange smell, a very toxic odour, a sort of perfume that wasn't. The reason for this was, the baker who supplied the soap to most of the bothies must have bought it in bulk - it was called rose petal, possibly a rambler according to how its perfume travelled - mind you, a great improvement on their boots.

Their water supply consisted of a bucket - with water usually drawn from a well and placed on a box or chair, usually inside the door. Sometimes there would be a tap at the horse trough, which meant horses were more up to date than the men.

To have a wash, this was done in a white enamel basin, quite a change from today with all mod cons.

Their toilet, in many cases, was very large - commonly known as the cattle court which on this occasion was the only time they shared their business with the livestock.

Like everything else, their lighting was very basic. Lights were fuelled by paraffin. The bothy would have a double burner lamp, the globe of which for colour was difficult to define, usually 50 - 50 black and white.

The heating and cooking facilities consisted of a large three-bar open fire raised a good height to allow for the build-up of ashes. They would also have a swee, which I already explained was a swinging bracket where they would hang their big black kettle or frying pan. That was when they had something to fry.

Pheasants and partridges all made good eating. A peewit's clutch is usually four eggs, hence, if there were only three, they weren't goggit, in other words, the incubation period hadn't started.

Their storage facilities for clothes and food consisted of two kists (chests). One was called a "mealer" for the food, which sometimes included silver fish; the other a "claser" for clothes.

Often they would put a sheet on the wall to hang up their suits, and cover them with another sheet. The walls of most bothies were treated with red and yellow ochre - a sort of distemper, and when it dried would leave a powder which at the least contact would attach itself to your hand, clothes or whatever.

Usually, if there were two men in the bothy they would sleep together in a double bed - not a very good arrangement, but your bed was there and you had to get into it. I would think quite an ordeal not knowing who your bedmate was to be, or his habits. Did he wet the bed, did he snore, walk in his sleep, think you were his wife? All the things you didn't want to happen.

Speaking about the wall-paint. If there were two in a bed, you always knew who was the senior. Not only did he sleep at the front of the bed, but there was no red colouring on his shirt from the wall at the back of the bed.

At this point I must mention the farmers' agreement with the bothy lads - their supply of coals, firewood, milk, oatmeal, liquid fuel for the bothy lamp, and, of course, their accommodation. Plus, as many potatoes and turnips as you could eat. They had small wages, but their perks were high.

No TV or wireless - what entertainment they had was made by themselves and also visiting lads from other farms. They would play their musical instruments, and possibly a game of dominoes or cards. Many a concert party was formed through a night in the bothy. Hence, today, they re-enact these times, forming a concert party called "Bothy Nichts."

Apart from these visits, the bothy form was a bench for all to use, but the residents sat on their own kists, their food chest, this being most used and nearest to hand.

Their bedclothes were washed by the farmer's wife, or the maid from the farm house. Their personal wash was usually taken home to mother, possibly once every two weeks.

The bed mattress was usually filled with one of the products from the threshing mill, the husks of the grain, called chaff. I called it a mattress, but it was really a large hessian sack. When first it was filled, you were three feet high, but after two weeks with the sweat and heat of the bodies it would be reduced to 12 inches. The procedure of filling the mattress was repeated approximately every three months.

Their main utensil was a bowl which was used for anything edible. Whether it was soup, fried eggs, tea, etc., it served the purpose. It was also a crime to wash your bowl from one six months to another. In fact, if a young lad in the bothy did such a deed, his senior would attend to the punishment administered for such a crime.

Another known punishment was administered if the young lad was caught while drinking his tea to have his spoon in his bowl. A crime had been committed and punishment was by his elder striking a hard blow with a spoon to the thumb that was holding the bowl.

When the utensil was really dirty, the mark of his thumb and where his lips touched the edge when drinking were very prominent.

A common trick played on the occupants would be to do a bit of what they called "lum stappin'. This was done by means of a hessian bag, soaked in water and pushed down the chimney. Needless to say, after a short period the bothy was filled with reek (smoke). At that point, all hell was let loose, but usually the pranksters had an advantage and escaped.

There was no covering on the floors, which consisted of flagstone or concrete. I can imagine when your feet hit the floor in the morning it was quite a rude awakening. Maybe there was method in the farmer's madness.

Rations were very meagre. Oatmeal played a prominent part, and was the basic diet in the form of porridge, bannocks, skirlie, brose, etc. Of course, there were potatoes and bread, and on the odd occasion sausages.

It used to be a common practice to cook a pot of porridge, pour it into a drawer which was lined with paper for the purpose, and allow it to go cold. This would be cut into slices and eaten at a later date. When their parents killed their pig, the bothy lads would receive enough bacon for a fry-up. To match the ham you required an egg, which was found in various places around the farm, usually known to the lads who, to save them being damaged in any way, as a gesture would remove them and drop them into the frying pan!

The man on the pin, if the horses were still in the stable over winter, had to feed all the others as well as his own pair, and take them out to the horse trough for their drinks. Another important task was to make sure each stall was cleaned out, and fresh straw bedding supplied. He also had to make the porridge in the morning preferably without any knots.

In the summer time, the man on the pin had it much easier. No stable duties as the horses were put out to grass. It even gave him time to re-straw his boots.

Their reflectory system (mirror) was usually put in place by a four-inch wire nail chapped into the wall ready for the cord or whatever to hang the mirror, which was usually about eight inches by five - either sitting on a ledge or hung by means of a piece of snare wire. This was a thin piece of stranded wire for snaring rabbits. Usually, if you tried to look in the mirror, to believe you had the measles would not have been an overstatement. Maybe a year's soap and water splashes were more obvious than the glass.

Shaving was a regular habit, at most once a week unless courting a young lady or a function took preference. Remember, shaving in those days was carried out by means of an open razor, sharpened by rubbing same on a leather strop. Quite an art to get a good shave. Possibly, the thought of the operation made them delay.

At some point I mentioned silver fish in the food chest (mealer). In case you haven't seen them, they were small insects, silver in colour and shaped like minute fish - harmless little things living on the flour, etc. A prank played was for some foreign bodies to be placed in the stovie pot when they had visitors. There were no plates - everybody gathered round the pot and supped. The prankster made a remark, "Now, boys, eat up - the one who reaches the bottom first gets the meat." After some fast eating they did. What he had done was put a rat at the bottom of the pot.

Food for thought. I suppose the next visit they would eat less. As Jimmy Cagney would have said, "O you dirty rat."

The Maid Threw Down The Towel

Another true story is about the maid in the farm house who, like many others, was kind to the bothy lads. For instance, when they went to collect their milk at the farmhouse, unknown to the farmer, she would place a lump of butter in the bottom of the flagon, then pour in the milk. When the cream formed on the top, no chance of detection - a nice perk.

This maid in particular would go that little bit further. When the farmer and his wife were away for the day, she would invite the bothy lads to the farmhouse for tea. The signal given was a single towel hung on the clothes line for the all-clear. The three lads were over the moon thinking about the farmhouse tea, The first lad, a bit earlier than the other two, walked straight into the parlour, only to find the farmer sitting in his chair. Needless to say, he made a hasty retreat to re-route his two pals. They had never noticed the maid had cancelled the visit by removing the towel from the clothes line.

This farmer, being a good sport, jokingly remarked to the ploughman, "How soon will we have to move out?" However, the butter was in safe hands.

One of the many games or tests of strength played in the bothy was called the swere tree. Two men sat own on the floor with the soles of their feet touching. They used the short handle that was made for lifting the sacks of grain when threshing on to the steelyard weighing machine, and gripped this with both hands. Pressing against each other's feet, they pulled until the winner pulled his opponent clear of the floor. This was considered one of the hardest tests of strength of any game they played, putting a good strain on the body.

Another test of strength was lifting two 56-pound weights above their shoulders. This type of weight was square-ish with a bar handle running through it. You would say that could be done with reasonable ease, but the catch was, the lift was carried out by using part of the hand - the pinkie. It was amazing how many could succeed in this test.

One Life Gone Eight to Go

The true story of three kittens . Mother cat gave birth to three unwanted kittens, causing a surplus of cats on the farm. In those days their method of extermination was to put the cat or cats in a hessian sack fixing the open end with a cord. This was usually a piece of binder twine used to bind the sheaves of grain from the horse drawn binder. After securing the sack with the three kittens inside the person concerned would find a deep pool in the burn and drop the sack in. Apart from its living cargo it would include a weight such as a fairly large stone. After being submerged for a period of time and long enough to drown the contents, they were removed from the water and buried in the fermenting bedding in the cattle court. The next day one of the farm workers was feeding the cattle when, to his amazement, thought he heard the sound of cats wailing coming from the direction of the dung covered floor of the cattle court. Investigating the sound and scraping away the muck he found the three kittens very much alive. The heat coming from the fermenting straw had given them a new lease of life. The kittens were reprieved, became handsome adults and roamed the farm buildings for many a year, getting their rations of milk in the Byre at milking time. What a sad beginning to what became a happy ending! You could say drowned *(downed)* but not out.

The Horse, His feed, His Shelter

I have written about the ploughman, his clothes and his housing. Now we come to the other part of the team, his pair of Clydesdales. Like the men, they were the champions of champions - a true and faithful friend, and when handled with care and kindness, would always be true to the master.

There was nothing worse than to see someone kicking or pulling the rein hard, thus hurting the horse's mouth. The bit is a piece of steel attached to the bridle, which went in through the horse's mouth and was the ploughman's steering column. He was supposed to give a gentle pull on the rein if he wanted his horse to go either way.

There was nothing better than to see these great animals being released for the first time into a field of beautiful green grass. The men would take them into the field and turn them to face the gate - the reason being they used to jump and kick with sheer joy. Now they were well away from any flying hooves.

Another pleasure was to pass a field where they were relaxing, swishing their tails for the flies, deserving every minute of their rest after a very hard winter's work. Their stable was a place of contentment on a winter's night. It was always very cosy, with these massive animals munching away at their fodder, a nice bit of hay with a lot of sweet clover. This was their main feed. There was a corn kist at the back of the stable which was the store for bruised corn - ears of corn fed through heavy rollers and flattened. Each horse got his measured ration from a small wooden box called a lippy.

Another memorable feature was the chain attached to his stall collar, a light type of bridle worn in the stable which went through a fixed staple on his hay hake, through what they called a sinker ball, either wood or steel. At the end of the chain was a T-piece, which went through the ball and kept the chain from pulling out, thus keeping the horse secure in his stall.

Speaking of stalls, no matter how many stalls in the stable, every horse would find his own. The ploughman always gave his horse first priority, then he looked to his own requirements.

It was great to be in the company of one of these men on a cold winter night when he would take a tit-bit for his pair, maybe a nice sweet swede neep, or a hot mash. Whenever he walked into the stable that welcome nicher would come from the stalls.

First of all, the lantern had to be lit. This was usually on a pulley and rope system. At one end, a small weight was attached to the rope, which was threaded through the pulley and clipped on to the lantern. When lighting or filling with paraffin, the light was pulled down and then raised clear of man or horse. You can imagine what would happen should an accident occur, with so much straw and hay, really inflammable materials lying around.

The shoes for a working horse would be what they call lifted - their feet pared and the same shoes refitted. A full set of shoes lasted six months. The horse's worst enemy was grass disease, and I believe still is today. I remember watching a nice young horse, four years old, die with grass sickness. It was in so much pain it was released from the stable into the cattle court to allow it to romp around. The pain was so bad there was no hope for this animal to live and I asked the question, "why couldn't it be put out of its agony"? The answer was that in those days, if you did that, the insurance company wouldn't pay up - the horse had to die naturally before payment could be made. It wasn't a pretty sight - anyone having witnessed it I'm sure would agree.

Yoking or starting time for the horseman was five o'clock to feed and groom their horses, and the usual mucking out. They would return to the bothy and have their breakfast, ready to start at 7.30. They finished on Saturday at lunch time.

During the harvest, they worked a 10-hour day for no extra pay - also four Saturday afternoons until 5.30 p.m.

Their agreement was done with a handshake when they were "fee'd" (employed) with a coin. The bargain was sealed if somebody accepted the 1/- paid by his new employer, the farmer. He would never go back on his word after accepting his arls (1/-). After six months, a single man could either be asked to stay or allowed to leave. If he was socht (asked), the signs were he was worth keeping, if not, he was allowed to leave. The ploughmen, when moving to another farm, used their horse and cart as a means of transport to move his kists. There is a story about a ploughman who arrived at this farm only to meet his new farmer who said, "You are the new man."

"Aye, I'm to be driving the fourth pair."

"Well," said his new boss, "Would you come and have a look at this field." As they entered, the farmer said, "If you take a look, you'll see a piece of land that hasn't been ploughed. Do you know what you call it?"

"Aye," said the ploughman, "It's 16 feet wide and it's called the end rig." The farmer replied, "Just remember, it's no' for standing on." In other words, don't stop.

That's what they said in the bad old days, so that the man ploughing or whatever wouldn't have to stop. If he was a pipe smoker he would fill two pipes in the morning and two at lunchtime in case the farmer caught him wasting time filling his pipe.

Through it all, an old ploughman of yesteryear still says, "They were the good old days."

There was a lot of competition, but a lot of comradeship as well. In this area of Angus many a married man had a little croft, maybe 12 acres, not enough to make a living, so he worked on one of the big farms with maybe five pairs of horses.

He couldn't afford horses or implements so the farmer would give his men permission to take his implements and horses to put in the crops. The men would repeat this with several crofts which were quite near to each other.

Today, unemployment is a very sore point - including the rural areas. If we give a thought to the amount of men employed on farms in yester year - one farm in this area had 28 workers with something like 16 pairs of horses.

In those days, there was no rural transport except a pedal cycle, which meant most of the food for human consumption was taken to the farms by horse-drawn vans - baker, butcher, greengrocer - even pots and pans, etc., were delivered by what they called a "pot an kettle man."

Then there were the cadgers selling herring, and fish in general, with possibly a box of apples, oranges, whatever.

I can recall the herring were sold at 1/- (5p) for a baker's dozen (13). In the season there was no better meal than herring and newly dug tatties from the garden.

Another source of food comes to mind - it was salted cod from Iceland - a massive fish which had been salted and dried. This was kept hanging outside, usually on what they called a fish hake, triangular in shape with several hooks for hanging the fish. Being salted, no insects would approach it, and not even the birds.

The housewife, when it was required, would cut off a piece. This would be soaked in water overnight to remove the salt, and it would be boiled then soaked in butter. A nice wholesome meal with chappit tatties.

Skirlie was another oatmeal dish consisting of onions, oatmeal, fat, etc., Simple but wholesome, mind you, a bit like what they used to feed to the chickens, called crowdie - even they had nothing to chuckle about.

Mistaken Identity

When times were hard and the single men in the bothy were poorly fed, porridge was their main source of food. This being so, should illegal rations such as hen's eggs come within their reach they were greatly appreciated. In this case the hen had laid her quota of eggs and after a short discussion it was agreed that needs must and the hen was next on the menu. They killed the hen which was laid to rest in the pot. The farmer who was rarely known to visit the bothy lads happened to pay them a visit. It was a little bit suspicious that there was something in the air. By this time the pot lid was having the occasional up and down movement meaning it was full steam ahead and that the hen had almost reached its destination - the bothy lads food bowls. The foreman and his companions, apart from starving of hunger, were disturbed that the farmer, still in attendance, would discovered his birds fate. Desperation was now upon them and as the farmer looked on the foreman grabbed the pot, looked at the farmer and lifted the lid saying, "Come oot what you may, ye gid in a rabbit." Aye, from feather to fur.

The Day The Thrashing Mill Cam In Aboot

This was a great occasion, along with the fact it meant two or three days' dusty hard work. The mill would arrive the night previous. It was put in position between the stacks or ricks. These had stood through the winter without allowing water or snow to cause any damage. This was due to the great art with which they were built.

When the grain was carted home from the fields, after being in stooks drying for a considerable time, it was transferred to the stacks.

The word "stack" meant a heap of hay, grain or whatever. The foundation was laid on stathels which were raised approximately 18 inches from the ground, thus allowing the air to circulate underneath, also to control the vermin which would climb up to the grain. No matter how they tried, there were still a lot of vermin at the thrashing. That's when the dogs had a gala day among the rats.

The great art in building a stack was to keep the hearting right, in other words, the centre. After the stack was built, they thatched it just like they do with a house roof. They took such a pride in this. To finish it they would trim around the edges, and place a corn dollie on top. This was an ornament made with straw.

When taking the sheaves from the cart to the stack and when it got too high, they would employ a pyter who stood on a ladder catching each sheaf and passing it on to the man building the stack - a pleasure to watch these craftsmen at work.

Back to the thrashing. The mill men as they were known, during the season worked day and night. When they arrived they had to set up the mill, meaning the machine had to be sitting level both ways. This was necessary to allow smooth running of what was called the drum, the part that travelled or rotated at a very high speed. Thus, when the sheaf was fed into the drum, it separated the heads of the grain from the straw, after which the grain went out the back of the mill where it was bagged.

Likewise, the straw came over the shakers, where the husks and the straw parted company. The straw usually was bundled ready for putting into a straw seu, a long straw rick. If it was wheat they were threshing the grain was put into large, heavy duty bags. When full they weighed two-and-a-quarter hundredweight.

That's when young boys became men. They would carry this from the mill, quite a distance up a stair to the grain loft where it was stored. Some of these men would be carrying twice their own weight. Quite a task, but it had to be done.

The mill was driven by a steam engine, which also pulled what they called the travelling mill from farm to farm.

Most farmers had their own fixed thrasher used for convenience thrashing. This was driven by a paraffin engine, usually a Shanks of Arbroath. To start this engine, it was heated with a blow lamp. It also had a single flywheel which, after the engine was heated, was pulled around when the engine started to run.

The straw from the inside mill was taken by elevator to the barn. These were at the highest point and could be controlled by regulating the openings at the various points.

When the travelling mill was at the farm, quite a number of staff were required to carry out this operation. They got helpers from the outlying farms; helping one another.

I must mention that a very important member of the squad was the louser, usually a lady, one of the wives who stood on the top of the mill with what they called a lousing knife. Her job was to pick up each sheaf, cut the binding string, and drop it into where the drum was running.

I can remember listening to the hum of the mill. If the louser over-fed it the tone completely changed - what they called chokin' the drum.

The mill men - those who travelled with the machine - would arrive at five o'clock in the morning to get what they called a head of steam, meaning the engine prepared for starting at 7.30.

Every farm they went to supplied the coals for the thrash, also breakfast at six for the mill men.

The machines were halted for a "mid-yokin'" when the farmer's wife brought out usually a buttery roll with home-made jam and a flagon of tea. For their dinner they would stop at 11.30 to 1 o'clock.

In the meantime, everybody went into the kitchen of the farmhouse for their thrashing dinner. I can still see the plates and their contents - usually a large plate of Scotch broth made with a bit of boiling beef which would be eaten with a piece of turnip, carrot and potato. To follow would be a massive plate of mince and tatties about the size of a barrow wheel! The sweet would be bread pudding or such like. I learned the meaning of eating like a horse, just watching.

Before all the above could take place, a lot of work had gone into getting the grain to this stage. The crop had to be cut. In the early days, the reaper was the fore-runner of the binder. This machine was invented by the Reverend Bell of Carmyllie, and was equivalent to the industrial revolution - a great leap forward from the days when grain was cut by the sickle, then the scythe. Now the reaper was a machine with flights or flails, and a cutter bar, just like the binder, but no means of tying the cut corn, or whatever, into bunches. This came much later with the binder.

The method used was by canvas cloths with wooden slats riveted on to same. As the corn was cut, it fell on to a canvas cloth running at right angles to the cut straw. A cloth on rollers running up the binder took it over the top. Another cloth took it down to the buncher and knotter, which was one of the cleverest pieces of machinery ever developed for the farm. This apparatus determined the size of sheaf by means of weight, after which it tied a piece of binder twine around the centre, cut the twine, and threw out the sheaf, helped by revolving forks. The clever part was, after it tied the knot, it cut and continued the string ready for the next sheaf.

Before this was invented, the grain was cut by the reaper and dropped off the back in little bunches which had to be bound and tied by hand. The bindings were several lengths of whatever grain was being harvested, which was twisted to make a binder, and that's where the binder had got its name, because it did just that.

Also attached was a board called a clapper board. This was placed at an angle with a backwards and forwards movement, leaving the cut ends of the sheaves with a taper effect. The reason for this was, when the sheaves were set up into the stooks in pairs they were put on the ground with the short side of the taper to the top, so that any rain would run from the sheaf on to the ground.

Another good idea - the twine for binding the sheaf was kept at the back of the machine in a small bin, allowing the twine to be kept dry, and, as it was used, run off the ball automatically. All together, a very clever apparatus.

When the harvest was all gathered in, the stacks were finished, the cornyard complete, all that had to come to complete the operation was the harvest home ball. This, I suppose, was a way of saying thanks, it's all over, home and dry. Following that there would be a harvest thanksgiving service in the village church. This included all fruit, vegetables, etc., all part of the general harvest. I'm sure the farmer had said, many a time, "Welcome home!"

Harvesting the Hay

When the hay was ready to cut in June month, it was said that the week of the Highland Show was the time for harvesting. It was cut by a mower like the binder, powered by a pair of horses and including a seat for the driver. This machine had nothing else but a cutter bar leaving the cut grass in what they called a bout. After cutting, it was left to win or dry, possibly having to be turned over allowing the air to filter through.

After this, there was another good invention, the trip rake. When the rake was full, the driver pushed a pedal which locked the wheels, allowing the rake to lift up and leave the hay in a heap ready for the next operation. This implement was called the Tumbling Tam. It was pulled by a single horse to the lines of hay collected by the rake. The Tam had teeth approximately five feet long protruding from the front in a wooden frame, and two handles with which the ploughman guided it.

When he had collected the fill of the machine, he made his way to the area where a cole was formed. A cole usually had what they called a centre boss made of wood, with three legs and spars, well-spaced, allowing the air to circulate and make the hay of a high standard. This was called a tramp cole, because one of the workers would walk around, tramping the hay to pack it into the side of the wooden boss keeping it well-packed and dry.

There was another type of hay cole, much smaller, without a wooden centre boss. This type, when being transported back to the farm, was carried on a hay bogie. This machine had very small wheels with a large, flat platform. At the front was a round drum the width of the platform, around which was a chain. This was pulled back and around the cole. The bogie tilted up, then the chain was wound up bringing the cole on to the platform. Once past the point of balance, the platform dropped, locking at the same time, ready for the journey to the farm.

The hay was then transferred on to a large stack by means of a hay fork. This implement had three pieces of metal which looked like large, bent needles. They were attached to a rope which went through a pulley on a tripod and attached to a yoke. The horse would then walk forward, closing the needles on the hay, at the same time lifting part of the cole on to the stack. This was a great labour-saving device. As the hay was lowered, someone would tramp round and round, making the stack compact and dry. This was the animals' main diet during the long winter.

On the subject of implements, there was the grubber. It had five or seven large spikes that loosened the soil previous to ploughing. It was pulled by a pair of horses and had two large wheels at the back and two small at the front.

This operation was carried out in winter when darkness fell very early. The man with the grubber seemed to have cats' eyes. If he was at the other side of the field from where you were, you couldn't see him or his horses, but if you listened you would hear "Squeak, squeak," coming from the wheels. Somebody said to the farmer, "Why don't you put some grease on the axles?"

"Na," was the reply, "if ye canna see them, ye can hear them, and ye know they're still working."

Even in the dark there was no hiding place!

A well-known horse breeder said to me, "And what I'm telling you applies to humans, animals, poultry, plants, etc. Never take a south horse north - always take a north horse south."

I've quoted that quite often, and in many cases it is true.

Today progress has taken over. No more squeaking grubbers to be heard, not even the ploughman's voice giving his commands to his gallant pair: "Hey WEESH!" or that click in the cheek telling them to go forward.

Never again will we hear the clink of the wooden cartwheel as it does its rounds - a sign it was in good working order.

Nor will we hear the sounds of the stable, the chain and ball going up and down through the hasp as the horses moved their heads when having their feed. The sound of hooves on the farm road as they pulled a neatly built cartload consisting of a five or seven ging load of sheaves to the stack yard..

That couthy welcome received when their master opened the stable door - and affectionate reply to kindness given.

But not forgetting that great breed of men, going out or coming home, sitting side-saddle on the horses.

Another of the memories - when you were passing the smiddy, the blacksmith would be very busy shoeing horses with the smoke from the burning hoof travelling upwards.

You could hardly see his face, and the air was full of the smell of burning hooves. Possibly two smiths were shoeing two horses, with another two pairs waiting to be done. The blacksmith was another man who deserves great praise for a job requiring great skill with plenty of brawn.

No more will we see the cornyard with stacks all neat and tidy, the familiar sight of the farmer's wife with the flagon of water and oatmeal (a mealy drink), also the buttery with jam at mid-yokin' (a break midway through the forenoon or afternoon). The meal and water was to cool down the blood when working amongst the hay - it was usually very hot, being June month.

Also silent is the steam engine that drove the threshing mill, which had that lovely hum as it separated the grain from the straw.

A nice sight was the hen and her chickens, balls of yellow fluff with mother always very busy teaching the brood how to guard against danger - with one cluck they scurried to her side. Sometimes they would disappear under her wings, with just the heads peeping through the feathers. These were the eggs that escaped the ploughmen's frying pan. After a thresh, flocks of birds would come to feed on the various seeds - green linties, yellow yites, shellies, blue juggies, speugs, etc. (the latter in their dozens), to name but a few - not forgetting the crows tearing off the theakin' (thatch) from the stack. Gone are the days.

The Cottar Kids
Tinkie Bairns And All Others

Having attended a country school, in this case, Colliston, in the centre of a very good rural area, and at that time a three-teacher school supplying a very good education if you took it on board.

The children travelled from the outlying farms, possibly walking three miles to the school, and likewise the return journey at night.

I've seen them arriving soaked to the skin and being allowed to try to dry their clothes on the metal guards around the classroom fire. This wouldn't be very effective, as most of the heat went up the chimney. Another part of the tedious journey were the roads - they encountered dust in the summer, and gutters (mud) in the winter.

Every Christmas there would be a concert for school funds. A lot of these children would take part. I used to have pity on them having their long trek home after the show, again by Shanks's pony.

The school had its own soup kitchen, the soup pot being the wash boiler fuelled by a coal fire. The ingredients were of the very best. Potatoes and vegetables were gifted by the farmers, while the rabbits, chickens, etc., came from various sources.

The soup cost 1d per bowl (240 old pennies made a pound), with one purchase per person. When collecting your bowl, which was made of tin, it was policy to make sure there were no dents, as a good bowl held more soup.

In addition to soup, a slice of dry bread was supplied from home, as it was said, "just to fill up another corner of that empty stomach."

The variety was very good:

Monday - pea soup
Tuesday - Scotch broth
Wednesday - tattie soup
Thursday - green kale (not so good)
Friday - rabbit or chicken.

I can see the cottar kids who had come a distance being so hungry that their slice of bread was consumed on arrival in the morning as a second breakfast. Not only did they travel a distance, but there were the tinkers' bairns whose parents would be encamped in some cattle rake for the summer months.

Their main industry would be making heather pot reenges, clothes pegs, etc., then they would come around the doors selling them, as well as safety pins, lavender, combs, anything they thought the housewife would need.

The men would offer to sharpen your knives, garden shears or whatever. In the summer evenings you could be sure to hear the skirl of the bagpipes, one of their clan hoping someone would pay the piper. It was said the real tinkers made good soldiers with many of them in the pipe bands.

I can still smell the aroma of the lavender coming from the large butter basket as the lady of the house was brainwashed about the tinkie wifie's hard-luck story, possibly three youngsters standing beside her, black faces and running noses acting the sad part. As thrifty as my Aunt had to be, she never put them away empty-handed, even if it was only a jam piece or a jam jar of tea.

In school, they were mixed through the class, and one boy sat beside me. His name was Murdo McLaren. One day he was bending forward on the desk, and I noticed a small insect crawling among his hair. It was easily spotted, because his hair was cropped bare, with a small tuft remaining at the front. Apart from that, he had a blue patch on his head which turned out to be gentian violet for ringworm. The crawly I saw was a louse crossing over the bare patch into the blue gentian.

Reporting when I got home, within minutes out came the bone comb and down went the newspaper. The first stroke of the comb revealed the truth - I had nits, in other words lice. The treatment started there and then.

A great thrill come the summertime, just before the holidays, was the school picnic to a place called Lunan Bay, approximately seven miles away from the school. This was the event of the year. Twenty-six farm carts painted in bright colours of blue, red, green, etc., their natural colours when new; horses and harnesses, with decorations looking their very best. They were box carts with what they called their tops - frames extended beyond the cart for carting sheaves of corn, hay or whatever. These allowed them to carry a much bigger load. For the picnics they filled sacks with straw and laid them over the tops, where the children sat with their feet in the bottom of the cart.

The morning of the picnic, as kids we were up early to see the parade of horses and carts arriving at the assembly point. What a thrill! - everyone dressed in their Sunday togs. I always thought it strange to see the ploughman sitting on the front of the cart fully dressed, when his usual was moleskin trousers, greaser, and complete with nicky tams.

It's all right admiring the finished article, i.e. horse and carts, but what about the hard work to get this show on the road - hours of tedious work just for the love of taking part.

On the day, you were told which cart was yours for the journey. The carter, on arrival, would draw a number - that told him where he would be placed in the parade. He also registered his name for the judging of the best turnout, the best dressed ploughman, and, of course, the best looking.

You may ask what happened if it rained - it was all in hand. Each cart carried a canvas cover. At the least sign it was rolled out with everybody underneath.

When we arrived at Lunan Bay two hours later, the children and parents went down to the beach. The ploughmen and their charges went to Redcastle Farm for stabling and feeding the horses. Should it rain during the picnic everybody adjourned to the grain loft at the farm where we played games and danced.

Usually, somebody would have a melodeon for accompanying the jigging. It doesn't bear thinking about - 26 horses and carts travelling at five miles an hour. Even the so-called good driver of today wouldn't stand it. Of course, different times - I wonder if for the better.

The picnic was very well organised. When you queued for your bag of goodies, it was girls and boys in their own line. The poakie (bag) contained:

1 sausage roll
1 Paris bun
1 cream cookie
1 cinnamon biscuit.

The liquid - a small bottle of explosive lemonade with the spring top and rubber washer. If you weren't quick enough when opening, half the contents were gone, there was so much gas in it.

The horsemen were supplied with a Forfar bridie, about the size of a horse's foot. If he took a bite in the centre, you could only see half his face. His liquid was a large screw-top of beer, and they certainly deserved it. When they drew for their number in the procession, number one was kept out of the draw. That was always the committee cart, possibly so they could have a dram or two en route under cover.

Another thing that made the day, you knew there were seven weeks' holiday ahead before returning to the skilee or slate pencil and slate, which was our jotter. The slate had a wooden surround to protect the edges. This required scrubbing regularly. When wiping your slate, a small piece of sponge was required. This was kept in a small box, like the one made of tin which held eight Oxo cubes when purchased. The only complaint after a short period, it stank to the high heavens.

Some pupils had their names burned into the frames of their slates, and great was the excitement at home when a new slate was bought, and the tip of the red-hot poker applied with the greatest of care.

Of course, we had jotters when a record had to be kept of your various tests.

When I think of how casual the school system was. The headmaster every Friday gave us an hour's talk on general knowledge, and he used to read jokes from the "People's Journal." Needless to say, we nearly died laughing, knowing full well if we didn't, no jokes next week. There was also a comedy short story called Meg and Andrew. The rural football teams were members of what they called the Progress League. He would keep us up to date with that.

I remember a person saying to a ploughman who had been out in the rain, his hair was really wet, "Aye, Jim, your hair's awfu' weet."

"Aye," he replied, "Ah'll hae tae get a wee tap on the heid."

I've just remembered an experience when walking home from the tatties sometimes through a stubble field, and feeling the water on your legs from the stubble. Being hollow, it held the rain. We might have been enjoying a piece of turnip stolen from the farmer, or some of the locust beans from the shepherd's store - feeding for his sheep.

Mixed with the locust beans was what was known as flake maize. I suppose you could say it was the fore-runner of corn flakes, at least to us young lads it tasted just as good. The beans were a bit sweet and satisfied our quest for food after one or two pieces.

When I was about eight years old I paid a visit to a field where they were ploughing, and, as today, there were always a lot of seagulls, crows, etc., taking the chance of the newly upturned soil which contains natural feeding for them.

The ploughman for some reason had accidentally killed a large herring gull. His girlfriend lived quite near the farm, and he asked me to take the bird to her and say he was very sorry, but he had killed one of Tam Swankie's doos (pigeons).

Having trekked the journey to the small farm where she stayed, I presented her with the doo. She looked at the bird with a very sad face, and, after careful thought, said, "Well, laddie, jist tak it back to him and explain it's a gull. Tam Swankie doesna keeps doos."

Back I went, and he, with a charming smile on his face, answered her statement by saying, "In that case, it's no good for eating," and he ploughed it into the ground.

It's amazing how easy you can be gulled by a doo.

The reason for the name "Swankie's Doos" is that Swankie is a prominent fisher name in the sea area of Arbroath, where the gulls are in their thousands.

As laddies, discipline was everywhere. People to give a wide berth included:

Number one - the headmaster. Not only during school hours, but wherever you met him. You never came face-to-face if you saw him first - that was when you made a fast exit. But, lo and behold, if he knew you had dodged his company by not saluting him, he would have a word in your ear in the morning. Unfortunately, he put it there with his hand. That was considered being insolent to your superiors.

Number two - another member of the cruel brigade was the village bobby. His method was opposite to the law - you were guilty until proved innocent, quite often by his own idea of corporal punishment. We noticed whether it be the bobby, the gamekeeper or the dominie (headmaster), for punishment they always went for your ears. Of course, it was the highest part - saved them from bending down.

How often I've heard it said, "You deserve a right bang in the lug for that" or "Wait till your father comes hame - he'll ca' yer heid aff." This left the young lad wondering what the situation would be like after his father had dished out the punishment and left him wandering around without his head. Or, "Wait till he comes home, he'll thrapple ye," or "Ye've maybe broken the skin on yer knees - wait till he comes hame, he'll brack baith yer legs."

Again, imagine your thoughts. Which hospital would be your destiny for broken legs?

Maybe it was "The best thing for you, my lad, is the cat o' nine tails." I used to look at the cat, and think, "My god, imagine a big cat wi' nine of them belting your back, with several miaows coming from the cat."

Another date on the calendar was Guising Night, not like today, when they mostly scrounge for money. In my day, you were disguised with false face and costume. If you received an apple or an orange, that was very much appreciated.

The highlight was dookin' for apples. Usually a washing tub was filled with water and the apples were put in. While they were floating on the top, you had to catch one in your mouth with your hands behind your back - a difficult task, but it could be done. Sometimes you were aided by a small fork in your mouth. If you were considered to have entertained the householders, you might receive a penny.

Another task bestowed upon me was the delivery of the evening paper to the Letham Grange Estate, which was approximately one-and-a-quarter miles door-to-door from where I stayed. In the dark nights, that lonely country road was frightening. It is said Rodger Bannister did the first four-minute mile. Sheer bunkum - I reckon the time I took was well within that, especially if the journey started with a noise in the wood. That was me off the blocks.

A mile down the road was the railway station, where, at 7 o'clock on the dot, a passenger train from Forfar to Arbroath would make a stop. I used to time myself to be there at that time. When it set off, its journey was parallel with the driveway to the mansion house where I was delivering. The reflection of the lights from the train seemed to give me strength to travel up this bush and tree lined avenue, approximately half-a-mile.

My imagination ran riot. When you heard a rustle coming from the bushes you imagined a huge stookie man on his way to grab you. Coming back the dark driveway was, to say the least, very eerie. Possibly a rustle in the bushes, just a rabbit scraping or a pheasant having a walk, but my mind never seemed to settle for something small - always monster size. I'm sure my footwear - what they called sandshoes - with crepe soles, were smoking by the time I got back to the village.

After going to bed, I used to imagine the queer things that could have happened on my journey in the pitch black.

There's one thing - a road accident was almost impossible, as there were few engine-driven vehicles on the road. It was amazing. We had no village street lights and never had a torch, but your eyes were adjusted to your natural surroundings.

One of my brothers who served in the 5th Airborne Division during the landings in various parts of the Continent had a discussion with me on how the darkness in his young life had served him well in battle. Eyes and ears were tuned as one. Even the breaking of a twig or similar put you on your guard. Another sense was that of smell. This seemed to be much sharper when brought up in the country.

Your feelings were also very good, especially on a winter's night, having a bath. The bath, being tin, was usually placed in the same room as the wash boiler, powst tub, etc., on a flagstone floor. The water got cold very quickly, so it was a case of in and out as fast as possible. When your feet touched the bare stone floor, the less time spent in its company the better.

Another treatment that was a must, the regular cleaning of your innernals, whether your bowels were clear or blocked, it was the same medication.

Every Friday night it was administered. We knew the medicine as "sinny pods." We didn't receive the pod, just the juice, after being steeped all night in water. The taste was so bad, we were coaxed into the trap of taking it with the promise of a spoonful of condensed milk. This was usually around 7 o'clock in the evening.

By 2 o'clock in the morning, the pains in your stomach were unbearable. Not only was it the worry of the pains, the next move looming ahead was the "watery" - another name for the toilet. This was placed what seemed a mile away, at the top of the garden. This stuff was as powerful as Semtex. It didn't move your bowels, it blasted them. Boy-oh-boy, I don't know how bad the pain is for a woman giving birth to a baby, but I can tell you in this case it must be like having twins. All that morning an the next day was sheer hell with stomach pains, but they always cleared up for church on Sunday, another voluntary job that said you must go.

I tell you, if anybody offered me a tanker load of condensed milk to take a spoonful of that terrible medicine, it would be no go.

The pods looked like what you see on a broom bush. We appealed for a change of medicine, something with a better taste. One appeal was granted, and the new medication was called cascarra. One week only, and we were back on the gelegnite.

I've never quite worked out whether this regular dose was good for you, or it may have been a way of saving food for one day per week.

The toilet paper consisted of the "Dundee Courier" cut up into little squares and hung on a wire nail. This had to be in plentiful supply ready for the dynamite run on Saturday when the effects were in full swing.

The church on Sunday was a "have to." I have nothing against religion, but there's one thing that I have never understood: as young laddies we attended The United Free Church, but in the village there was also the Old Church - the two within 500 yards of each other. When making our way to the service, we would meet some of my own school pals heading for the other church, but you never recognised each other. That order must have come from both sets of parents. In other words, pals all the week, enemies on Sundays.

After church, there was a rule, if you were going for a family walk it was in order to retain your Sunday best clothes - if not, you put on your old clothes and remained at the back of the house where you would not make contact with the outside world.

A trick I learned was the penny we got to put in the church plate for the collection I always felt was unfair - they got a penny, I got nothing. So I worked out a system. We got what we called a Saturday's penny, of which I would spend half - that left me with a halfpenny which I gave to the church and retained the Sunday penny for self.

You could comment, why didn't somebody see you put the halfpenny into the collection box? It was very simple. In the pew, which had a seating capacity of eight, there would be my four brothers, my sister, and our grandfather. They used to think I was very keen on church. I made sure I was in the seat first, not to be religiously saved, but from freezing to death - as the hot water pipes were at the end next the wall. The type of collection unit was a square box on the end of a long handle. This reached the full length of the pew. You've heard of when the penny dropped - in this case when the halfpenny dropped, with just the box as a witness, it being well out of sight of my grandfather.

Transport was non-existent, there were no buses and the train station was a mile-and-a-quarter away. If you had to see a doctor, dentist or whatever, we walked into town and back, a round trip of eight miles. If you weren't feeling too good it was a long trek, especially if it was raining or snowing. A visit to the doctor in those days cost you 7/6 - that was a lot of money when wages were approximately 40 shillings per week. That's why the doctor wasn't needed until desperation crept in. The first time I went to the dentist to have a tooth extracted it cost a shilling, which included the torture - I mean the needle in the gum which never seemed to take much effect at the time, but on reaching home, you could neither feel your gum or your face.

Delayed Action

We must not forget the strap, that piece of leather kept in the dominie's pocket, that was commonly known as the persuader. This lump of leather called the tawse, had four tails on the end of it. When this was about to be applied, you were asked to hold out your hand. The dominie then lifted his arm above his head, the strap fully extended in his hand, ready for the downward stroke, and, boy, when a movable object hits an immovable object at full force - result, a very sore hand. This depended, of course, on how many he thought you could take before he took your life. The word "corporal" seems to creep in here, but this man's power being such, I would rank him Brigadier. After rendering his client six of the best, the victim would naturally use mother nature's release valve and scream his head off. To add insult to injury, he would shout, "Stop that nonsense - what are you crying for?" To think he in his anger administered the punishment to the extent where the recipient's hand was as near to amputation as it would ever be, and he asks, "What's wrong with you?"

I remember one big lad who was condemned to six of the best. He accepted one, and decided that was enough. When the dominie brought the belt down the next time, he pulled his hand away before contact was made, grabbed the belt, threw it the full length of the classroom, then proceeded to strike the headmaster. He went back to his seat and no further action was taken, but later he was expelled from the school.

It was discovered later that his hands were already blistered with whatever work he was doing in the evenings on his father's croft. It was rather strange, he who was going through hell, and the name of the small croft was Paradise.

Guddling for trout on a late spring day was quite an art. You would lie on your stomach at the side of the burn, gently put your hands into the water, maybe two feet apart. You would then bring them together very slowly underneath the overhang of the bank, the place where the trout would rest in the shade, and feel very gently until you got a tickle - that's when the trout was in your hand. At the right moment, you closed your hands, at the same time throwing the fish on to the bank. One thing that stands out in my mind was the lovely smell of wild mint, the plant being crushed with the pressure of your body and giving out its odour.

Tales of the river bank apart from the trout - you could listen to the birdsong, the bleating of the sheep, maybe a sparrow hawk diving on his prey - or the skylark rising upwards giving his all in song, or, as they say, singing like a lintie - but above all the sound of the water rippling over the stones. The water was so clear. If you were thirsty the first thing you looked for was a gravel bed where it was safest to drink the water, it having been cleansed running through the gravel. Your drinking vessel was your hands, which you used as a scoop.

Another thing we searched for was a plant called a Lucy Arnot. The flower was white with one single bloom, the same type of flower as hemlock, but with a cluster-type head. Once we found them, it was a case of digging at the base of the stem, where you would find a large nut which we used to eat. We knew them as pig nuts (truffles).

Back to the trout - when guddling, there was one thing that we were frightened of - that was the water rat, whose habitat was in the huddles of the bank. I have seen a guddler give an almighty scream, at the same time lifting his hands out of the water with a rat's teeth firmly embedded in his finger. Needless to say, they usually dropped to the ground soon after surfacing. The cure was home to the first aid cabinet, where the lady of the house dressed the wound by applying lashings of iodine - more painful than the rat-bite!

The Pig Killing

The married men usually kept two pigs. After they were fat, they would sell one and keep one for their own use. This was a special day, and a great occasion when the pig was killed. The pigs were twice the size they kill today, more like a young bullock - well . . . just about!

Each cottar house had its own swine's kray, a small pig house where they were fattened. On the big day, the killer would arrive, usually a local man who specialised in this art. The proceedings started with the man with the knife stepping into the kray with a rope. At one end was a loop which he laid flat on the floor. Coaxing the pig to move around until its foreleg was over the loop.

He pulled the loop tight, and, hey presto, the pig was caught. The door of the pig's dwelling was then opened, allowing the animal to walk into the open space, where two burly chiels would slide legs over its back. Needless to say, usually the pig didn't like it and complained profusely, by squealing its head off. Their job was to manoeuvre its head into position for the killer to stun it with a big hammer.

I remember seeing such an act go wrong. Instead of being hit dead in the centre of the head, it was struck in the eye. At this very rare instance, cruelty was in the air.

After the killer managed to slit its throat and having cut the main artery, the pig was allowed to rise and walk - the idea was that the heart pumped the blood out. When the animal was drained it dropped to the ground.

The plotting tub was next on the menu - this consisted of half a wine barrel and by this time it was filled with near boiling water. The pig was then laid into the boiling water. After a short period the helpers, having been issued with sharp scrapers, took the hair from the skin.

Having removed the body from the tub with great difficulty, it was then strung up on a ladder, where its intestines were removed. These were caught in a tin bath used for washing day, where they were separated. Some were destroyed, and others kept for various uses.

The carcass was then allowed to hang for a period of time to cool, after which it was split up the middle and removed to the kitchen where it was surveyed by the killer, who proceeded to cut it up into the various hams, etc.

The head was boiled and processed into potted head; the "puddings" or intestines were turned outside in, cleaned of excrement and sterilised, ready to be filled with oatmeal, onions, sage, whatever. The result - mealy puddings. It was common banter among the ladies that so-and-so had a recipe for making the best puddings.

The hams that were to be kept for later, having no deep freeze, had to be preserved with salt and brown sugar - the salt to preserve, and the sugar to sweeten the bacon. They were wrapped in muslin - the reason for the covering was to keep off flies, and to absorb any brine dripping from the hams.

They used to say if it dripped on your head, it caused a bald patch. Mind you, when I think back, there were an awful lot of bald ploughmen!

Another part that was in great demand was the bladder. The young boys on the farm were presented with it by the killer. It was dried and transformed into a football. Possibly short-lived if treated roughly, nevertheless a novelty of the time.

The hams were hung on big hooks fixed in the kitchen ceiling, and used as required.

Well, another day, another pig - the one that stayed at home and never got boared *(bored)*.

The Only Time They Left The Land

Story Time!
This story goes back to the days when farm labourers knew nothing but hard work, and holidays were just a dream. As in my young day, the only things that mattered were food, clothes, and a roof over your head. That was the holiday.

The couple in this instance were lucky having entered a competition to promote margarine. They received notice of their success which was a flight for two to Canada, also a lady's and a gent's Raleigh three-speed gear bicycle.

As they studied the situation, his wife didn't say much, but was deep in thought, thinking to herself, "I haven't left the farm for 20 years, and I haven't ridden a bike for the same time - and now, Canada here we come!"

Looking at her husband, she said, "Ye ken, Jeem, the bit aboot fleein' tae Canada was just a kid on. Juist hoo lang will it take us on wir bikes?"

"Na, na, lass," he said, "The air tickets are in the post."

The great day arrived, when they were ready to leave the land for the first time. Having bought his wife a nice new dress, a lovely dark blue with white collar, he was standing with her outside the lounge at the airport thinking how lucky they were, an having a good look at the unfamiliar surroundings.

At this point, a large seagull flew over and dropped its cargo on Meg's shoulder an down the front of her new dress. She, in her broad Angus accent, looked at her husband and said, "Jeem, dinna stand there gowkin', see a piece of paper."

He replied, "Ye needna bather, the bird'll be miles awa by this time."

After the shock had passed, she said, quietly, "Well, Jeem, they say it's lucky, but I didnae want as much as that."

At last the time had arrived to board the plane, and to say they were apprehensive of the new experience was an understatement, having been given a lot of advice from the various know-alls who had never flown, about being sick, the turbulence, etc.

Having no mod cons on the farm, she got to thinking, what if it's an outside lavatory? She even speired at Jeem, if the watery was inside. To counter the various discomforts now embedded in her mind, her hand luggage contained health salts, soor plooms, brandy balls and every cure for every ailment that would affect them on the trip.

Now they were on their way, the pilot having had a word with his passengers to put them at their ease.

By this time, they had travelled 300 miles, when the pilot made an announcement that if they cared to look out the starboard window they would see one of the engines was on fire. There was no problem - he would extinguish it from the cockpit, and could still land on three engines.

Meg looked at Jeem with terror in her eyes, saying, "Look here, is it no' time to get oot o' this thing?"

"Na, na," was the reply, "Ye heard what the driver said."

Another 300 miles and the same announcement, but this time it was the port side. Meg was now doing her nut and said, "Nae wonder they gave us a bike each, the wye this thing's brackin' doon."

A short time later, the pilot made another announcement to say his last port engine was on fire, but that everything was all right.

Meg looked at Jeem and said, "If that last engine conks out, does it mean we'll be up here a' nicht?"

On the return journey, everything went smoothly until they were coming in to Edinburgh. Jeem said to her, "Ye're wonderin' if we're near hame. Ging across tae the other side of the plane and look oot the window and you'll see the airport."

As she got there, the pilot banked the aircraft. She scrambled back to her seat and said, "Jeem, ye should never have telt me tae dae that, especially wi' my wecht."

The Farmer Nailed the Apprentice

The joiner was sarking boarding a cart shed roof, when the farmer, who had been spying . . .

By the way, this was a common practice when the tradesmen were working on farm buildings - having been there, I know!

For instance, a skylight in the roof of an adjoining building looked quite an innocent piece of glass. You thought your imagination was running riot when a further look confirmed the appearance of the farmer's head, complete with beady eyes sending a message to his brain - sorry, to his built-in system of conniving doubt.

. . . back to the apprentice. In those days, the receptacle for his nails was a white apron, which, when folded a certain way became a hold-all. In this case, a hole had developed, and as the apprentice moved, the nails were falling to the floor.

The farmer looked up, pointing his badge of office, a walking stick, saying, "Here, laddie! You're losing a lot of nails!"

"Aye, farmer," he replied. "If I were you I widna worry too much - you'll find them all, in your account."

Sixteen Years with no Remission

(It just happened) in this case to the maid on the farm. The bothy lad who drove the second pair of Clydesdales on this farm courted the maid from the farm house. After a while she intimated that she was expecting a child. He at this point became, to put it mildly rather disturbed with this sudden shock stating he would require two or three days to think it over. She replied saying, "You didn't need that when you carried out the act." Having waited for weeks and months for him to appear and tell her what he had decided, it was all in vain. Sadly she never saw him again, so sought legal advice and was awarded an allowance of 7/6 per week to be paid by the party concerned until the boy was 16. When the boy was old enough he was sent by his mother to the neighbouring farm to collect the 7/6 every week. This continued until he was sixteen. On this occasion his mother told him that this was the last time he would have to collect the money, and to be prepared for some remark from his father. Sure enough he handed his son the payment saying, "Son, it has nothing to do with you but tell your mother and watch her face when you tell her that this is the last payment." "Well dad," he replied, "This has in a way nothing to do with you, but my mother gave me a message to tell ye, and I've to watch your face when I tell ye." "Ye were never the father ata."
In other words what you might say 'paying into the wrong account'.

Twelve and a Tanner a Bottle

Speaking with an old timer who worked Clydesdales all his working life, from the day he left school at the age of 14, he told me his wages were 10/- (50p) for a five-and-a-half day working week. He happened to remark that at that point in time a bottle of whisky cost 12/6, which meant you couldn't buy a bottle from your week's wages.

In comparison with today, on average, you could purchase 10 bottles anyway.

Where is the problem? Are the wages too high, or is the whisky too cheap? Teetotallers, please note, this doesn't apply to you.

The Birds and the Bees

Nae Problem With These Down On The Farm
The heading can be misleading - in this instance very much so. My great friend had a fairly large farm with a lot of breeding stock - cattle, sheep, etc.

Our families were just about the same ages, Mr and Mrs X having three boys, and my wife and I three girls. Should the topic of discussion of education crop up, the most difficult area was the facts of life, old mother nature and how we would be able to cope should we be asked a straight question, such as "Dad, what is sex?"

I admitted my knowledge was like most married couples, but the difficulty with me was transferring the facts of life without embarrassing myself or my family with some contrived fairy tale, such as, they came from a cabbage, or that a stupid bird delivered them.

First of all, I don't grow cabbages. Secondly, Angus seems to have a low supply of this type of bird. And, being an undertaker, I should be the last person to discuss life or how it came about - my problem was where we are going.

Explaining my difficulty to my farmer friend, he said his problem was made much easier by having the animals to refer to, and that an early age would introduce his boys to the happenings in the animal kingdom, such as the birth of a calf, a lamb, piglet, etc.

This subject was never in the conversation for a considerable time, until one of his young boys he thought was ready for the first lesson. Having a cow due to have her calf, he said to his young lad, aged four years approximately, "Put on your boots and we'll go and attend to the cow giving birth."

When they arrived at the byre she had started calving, and doing well, with the head and front legs on the way to their new world. The young lad looked at his father and stared in sheer amazement at the calf, and asked, "Dad, how did that get in there?"

Father: No comment.

Still on the simple method of sex education, walking through the animals on the farm at a later date, the wee lad and his dad were going through the breeding stock, when, like a bolt from the blue, the wee lad said, "Dad, how do you have that bull amongst the cows?"

"You see," came the reply, "If we didn't do that, we wouldn't have any calves."

Again the boy spoke, "How do you have a ram amongst the ewes?"

Very simple question, simple answer: "If we didn't, we wouldn't get any lambs."

At this point, he said to me later, I was in his thoughts, having no animals to make it so easy to educate the youngsters on the facts of life. When, as they were arriving at the farmhouse his educational world crashed at his feet. The same lad had been silent for quite a while, then he turned to his father and put the million dollar question, "Dad, I've been wondering, how do you and mum sleep together?"

Father, now back to basics, could only answer after careful thought, "Now then, son, I think you had better ask your mother."

Another tale, in a similar vein, concerned the young son of a crofter from one of the Glens. To get to school, he boarded the bus at 7.30 in the morning, returning at 5 p.m.

This morning, he requested his best Sunday clothes, best shoes, good slag of his father's hair cream - and just a spot of perfume behind his ears.

As he was eight years of age, his mother was beginning to have doubts about the various requests, so she put the question to him, "What goes, with the hair cream, etc?"

He replied, as the schoolbag was placed on his back, an he was heading for the door, "It's nothing to worry about, we're having a sex lecture." Leaving his mother to think it out, he was on his way.

The day went past, with his mum wondering what to expect on his return. On time as usual, the bus stopped. He came rushing through the door, very upset, throwing his cap in the corner of the room, likewise his shoes, next his best clothes.

With that look of disappointment on his face, his mother, taking control, said, "What's all the fuss about? I thought you were having a sex lecture." He replied, "It was terrible."

"What went wrong?"

"It was only theory."

That must have been disappointing at eight years of age.

The Farmer and the Fire Brigade

An elderly Angus farmer had been to the market to see his cattle being sold, with good results, good enough to partake of a whisky or two. On returning to the farm, he discovered smoke belching from his steading. He immediately phoned the emergency services. The girl at the other end of the phone asked if it was an ambulance or whatever.

He replied, "If it puts out a fire, just send it."

When the first engine arrived, the driver jumped out, and found the farmer standing in amazement. He was coloured, something very unusual in the farming areas.

Gazing at him, the farmer asked, where do you come from?

The driver replied, "Pakistan."

"By god," said the farmer, "that just shows the speed of these modern machines. You're here before the Brechin boys!"

To Be a Farmers Boy

The sun had set behind the hill, across the dreary moor,
When weary and lame, a boy there came, up to a farmer's door.
"Can you tell me wherever there be
One that will me employ?
To plough and sow, to reap and mow,
And be a farmer's boy?
And be a farmer's boy?"

The farmer's wife cried, "Try the lad. Let him no longer seek."
"Yes, father do," the daughter cried, while the tears rolled down her cheek.
"For those who would work, it's hard to want,
And wander for employ.
Don't let him go, but let him stay,
And be a farmer's boy
And be a farmer's boy."

The farmer's boy grew up a man, and the good old couple died.
They left the lad the farm they had, and the daughter for his bride.
Now the lad which was and the farm now has
Often thinks and smiles with joy
And will bless the day he came that way
To be a farmer's boy
To be a farmer's boy.

Oor Auld Porridge Pot

When we were wee bairnies a' rinnin' aboot,
Oor porridge was made day in an' day oot
By the kind hand o' mither, wha stirred in the meal
In a cantie bit pottie that suited us weel.

Hoo aft ha'e I looked on its metal wi' pride,
While watching my mither I stood by her side,
And got my first lesson in cooking sae fine
The gudely hame dish on which true Scotties dine.

"Noo lassie," she said, "see and boil them richt weel,
Keep stirrin' aboot, or ye'll lump a' the meal."
I aye did my best to obey her command,
But only succeeded in scalding my hand.

Thae days noo are gane, the lads a' are men,
The lassies grown up, some wi' hames o' their ain,
While the three-legged pot which did duty for a'
Is noo painted and gilded and looks unco braw.

Though crackit it still can adorn wi' grace,
In the porch at oor hame we ha'e gien it a place,
Wi' a flo'erpot inside, an' the flo'ers look sae fine,
Ye never wad think it made porridge lang syne.

So noo a' you lassies just startin' in life,
Wha began 1930 as a new married wife,
When furnishing braw, though it be but a cot,
Be sure mang the lave get a gude porridge pot.

Memories

We met, we married a long time ago,
We worked for long hours when wages were low,
No TV, no radio, no bath - times were hard.
Just a cold water tap and a "walk down the yard."
No holidays abroad, few carpets on floors,
We burned coal on the fire, and didn't lock doors.
Our children arrived, no pill in those days,
And we brought them all up without any State aid,
They were safe in our lanes, and could play in the park,
And old folk could go for a walk after dark.
No valium, no drugs, and no LSD,
We cured most of our ills with a good cup of tea.
No vandals, no muggings - there was little to rob,
We felt we were rich with a couple of bob.
Milkman and farmer, would whistle and sing,
A night at the pictures was one big mad fling.
Now we're alone, and look back through the years,
We don't think of bad times, the troubles, the tears,
But remember the blessings - our home and our love,
And that we have shared them, we thank God above.

Hot Feet

or *Time And Tide*

The young ploughman went to the foreman to explain that his feet were so hot and blistered he could hardly walk. He removed his boots and socks.

The foreman looked and said, "Laddie, you've got what they call bothy lad's feet. The only cure is salt water straight from the sea."

The lad, looking slightly dismayed, asked, "And where is this sea?" The farm being 16 miles from this precious water. The next question was: "How do I collect it?"

His senior advisor explained that you had to cycle and take a bucket. "When you arrive at the harbour at Arbroath you'll see an elderly gentleman sitting on the harbour wall. Ask him for threepence worth of sea water."

The lad did as he was bid and cycled all the way back to the farm only to discover that he had spilled all the water. He confessed to the foreman, who told him to go back to Arbroath, but this time take a bucket with a lid.

On arrival at the harbour he found the water salesman - **but the tide was out.** Asking for another bucketful, and paying his three pence, he said in amazement to the old man, "My goodness ye've selt an affa lot o' water since the last time I was here last!"

The Tail of a Stable Rat
(A true story)

This story was told by a blacksmith in the days when horse shoeing was part of his everyday life. In this case, the stable was occupied by 24 horses which were used for contracting work in the town and surrounding district.

Should some of the horses require their feet attended to, the rest went out to work while the others were left behind for the blacksmith to collect. They would be taken to the smiddy to have their feet pared, new shoes fitted, or whatever.

The smith was returning the horses to the stable when he noticed something very odd on one of the shelves where the various materials were kept.

There was harness polish and the dandy brush for grooming, etc. In this case it was a bottle of linseed oil without a top which was receiving special attention from a rather large rat.

This bottle was on the bottom shelf of two, and the rat was trying very hard to get at the contents, but with very little success.

Not to be beat, he climbed up to the top shelf, which had a space of about seven inches from the one he had just left. To the blacksmith's surprise, the rat proceeded to hang his body by his front feet and at the same time drop his tail into the open bottle.

When his tail was saturated with oil, he pulled his whole body on to the shelf, completing the operation by drawing his tail through his mouth and so drinking part of the contents of the bottle.

Hence the saying, thereby hangs a tale - well oiled, at that.

The Horseman's Word

THE Horseman's Word is the mystical phrase which gives total control over horse and woman. It was revealed only to initiates into the secret Society of the Horseman's Word which was at its peak between 1850 and 1930.

The Society was strongest in North-East Scotland but extended as far south as Norfolk and Suffolk. Its roots lay in a horse cult imported from the Continent in the Dark Ages, and by Medieval times the Society of Horsemen ranked as a secret craft alongside that of millers and masons.

Freemasonry became open to non practising masons around 1717, and about the same time technological advances rendered the millers' secrets obsolete. However, three events helped to advance the Horsemen and make their society the longest surviving secret trade craft.

The first was the breeding of the Clydesdale horse from six Flanders stallions imported into Scotland by the Duke of Hamilton in the mid-18th century. The second was the invention of the two horse swing plough, and the third was the Napoleonic Wars which required vastly increased agricultural output.

From about 1820 onwards the Clydesdale horse replaced oxen as the Principal farm work beast, and from 1850 the Society of the Horseman's Word rose in power and prestige. It was helped by the farm-toun system of Scotland where a small community was grouped around a farm. Farm workers in England tended to live in villages away from their place of work, and this, and the savage restrictions on agricultural trade unions, prevented the same expansion.

Membership of the Society was essential for any youth wishing to rise in the strict, social farm hierarchy. Unless he was an initiate he could not become a ploughman, nor, could he court farm servants. He would begin work at the age of 14 in charge of the cows, and by 16 he would be given the spare plough team, and on his 17th birthday would find on his pillow an envelope containing a single horse hair.

This was his invitation to join the Society, and one he dared not refuse. A ballad from the North East tells of his progression:

Syne I got on for baillie loon,
Syne I got on for third,
Syne I had to get of course,
The Horseman's grippin Word!

The initiation ceremony was usually carried out at Martinmass, and had to be attended by 13 novices. Each was required to bring a jug of whisky, a loaf of bread and a candle, all purchased with difficulty from his meagre six monthly fee. His sponsors, usually the older ploughmen on each farm, would lead the youth blindfolded to a barn at midnight. They would stop before the closed doors and the senior Horseman, would give a measured knock and a whinny like a horse. From inside came the question: "Wha telt ye to come?"

"The Deevil", was the reply.

"Which wey did ye come?"

"By the hooks and crooks of the road"

"By which licht did ye come?"

"By the stars and licht of the moon"

"How high is your stable door?"

As high as taks the collar and the hames"

"Where were ye made a Horseman?"

"In a Horseman's Hall where the sun never shone, the wind never blew, the cock never crew, and the feet of maiden never trod."

When the interrogation was complete the door swung open to admit the initiates. The youths were stripped naked and forced to kneel before a makeshift altar formed by an upturned sack of corn. The presiding Horseman set them numerous catechisms and before administering the oath would question them: "What is the tender of the Oath?"

"Hele, conceal, never reveal, nor write, nor dite, nor carve, nor write in sand", The youths would chant. Then they repeated the Horseman's Oath and swore never to reveal the secrets they would learn "... and in failing may my body be quartered in four parts with Horseman's knife and buried in the sea 40 fathoms from the shore where the tide ebbs and flows every 24 hours, or may I be torn to pieces by wild horses." Each youth was then plied with whisky and taken to a corner of the barn where the Horseman's Word was whispered in his ear. Then he was led befuddled to the darkest, innermost recess of the barn where a horned, shaggy figure sat on a corn stook with cloven foot outstretched.

The youths would tremblingly shake the hand of the Auld Chiel before being led out. More and more whisky was passed round until the youngsters were stupefied. The older men raised their jugs in a final toast:

"Here's to the horse with four white feet, The Chestnut tail and mane, A star on his face and a spot on his head, And his master's name was Cain."

The youth would be carried back to bed and roused a few hours later for the normal 5 a.m. start. He would now be allowed to lead out the first team to prove he now had total control over the most powerful horses. The farmer usually watched in disgruntled silence, knowing he now had to pay the youth a man's wages. He knew, too, that neither he nor any member of his family would ever be allowed into the Society. Such was the superstitious awe in the secret Society that disputes were rare between men and master. The farmer also knew that only initiated Horsemen could work the fields. Those who weren't would find the farm horses refusing to leave the stable. Much of the initiation ceremony, which continued in this form to at least the 1930's, reeks of witchcraft. The 13 initiates, the shaking of the Auld Chiel's foot (the Devil), the parody of a religious ceremony, and lastly, the spells cast over horse and woman. The persecution of witches in the 17th century simply drove witchcraft underground, and this surviving element of the old pre Christian religion found a last refuge amongst the isolated farming communities of North- east Scotland.

Once a youth had been initiated his studies continued for at least five years. He was taught how to administer certain drugs. He was taught that toad's blood and pig's dung are totally repellent to horses. If smeared on a stable door the horses would refuse to leave. Similarly, a small nail placed under a collar would turn the calmest horse wild. By such means the Horsemen ensured that only they could work a farm's horses.

One trick, demonstrated on a few occasions, was to plant a fork in a dung hill and hitch a team to it. The Horseman urged the horses forward. Their muscles bulged but the fork did not move. It seemed like magic to the watchers - unless, of course, the Horseman was holding a totally repellent object right beneath the horses' nostrils!

Much of the Horseman's control over horses seemed like magic to those initiated although most of it was simply the ancient art of horsemanship handed down from prehistory. The reason a new initiate could handle the powerful first plough team was due to the senior horseman on the farm placing an oatcake made from oils of origanum, rosemary, fennel and powdered pad beneath his armpit as he lay in stupefied sleep. This was removed before he woke and surreptitiously broken beneath the horses's nostrils before he led them out. The aromatic spices cleared the smell of the previous handler and replaced it with the odour of the youth.

This concoction was first mentioned by the Roman writer Pliny as a love potion, and it was certainly believed Horsemen were irresistible to women. This may explain the high illegitimacy rates in the Northeast earlier this century or to say you had been courted by a Horseman would bring nods of understanding rather than condemnation. Confidence in courting, however, has always proved successful, as has confidence in handling animals!

There is no doubt the horsemen of yester year had an amazing control over horses to an extent never seen today.
Increased farm mechanisation from 1930 onwards saw the gradual demise of the Society of the Horseman's Word although it does still survive in outlying parts of the Northwest and Caithness and the age old secrets are still passed on.

As to the Word itself it is believed this is the phrase "Both as One", signifying total empathy between horse and man This derives from our Celtic forebear who pushed west on the Continent in the first millennium B.C. riding small shaggy ponies with such consummate skill they appeared part of their mounts and created the legend of the half man half horse centaurs.

Was it all just confidence and ancient "tricks of the trade" or did something much older lie behind it?. The Society of the Horseman's word did extend as far south as Norfolk and Suffolk and here individual ploughmen were initiated by passing Scottish horsemen. A book or rural Norfolk in the 1930's says man were unable to cope with the secrets revealed to them without support. A few committed suicide while others had hallucinations about giant Clydesdale horses entering their bedroom. Only those with the Horseman's Word today will really know what lies behind it.

Reduction in farm servants wages
April 1931

The annual feeing market for married farm servants, which was held at Arbroath on Saturday, attracted large crowds of agricultural workers to the town from a wide radius in the county. Very few engagements were made, however, and it was evident that there is to be a considerable reduction in wages. The general reduction, according to the terms accepted on Saturday, would be about £10 per annum, or 4s per week, on the present rates. The wages for grieves were about £75; for foremen, £63; for married horsemen, £60; for cattlemen, £65; for orramen, £63; all with the usual perquisites.

Three, 3 Horse binders - Arrat Farm, Angus

4 pairs ploughing at Arrat Farm led by Andy Church

Agricultural Wages (Regulations) (Scotland) Act 1937

District No. 10 Agricultural Wages Committee hereby give notice that they propose to fix minimum rates and minimum overtime rates of wages for workers in agriculture for time work in the district comprising the counties of Lanark, Renfrew, Dunbarton, Stirling, Clackmannan, Bute (except Arran and Cumbrae) and Perth (the western area so far as included in the parishes of Ardoch, Dunblane and Lecropt, Kincardine, Kilmadock and Port of Menteith).

These minimum rates, which are summarised below, will come into operation at a date to be fixed by the Scottish Agricultural Wages Board and will continue in operation until further notice. The minimum rates proposed in the case of male workers are as follows:

Shepherds - 21 and over 37/- per week; **18** and under **21, 34/-** per week; **15** and under **18, 28/-** per week. theses sums are to be increased by 1/6 per week for each dog which the shepherd is required by the conditions of his employment to keep and feed.

Byremen and Cattlemen, Pigmen and Poultrymen - 18 and over, 37/- per week; under 18, 28/- per week.

Ploughmen - 21 and over, 37/- per week; 18 and under, 34/- per week.

All other Male Workers (except casual workers and milkers) - 21 and over, 35/- per week; 18 and under 21, 32/- per week; 15 and under 18, 26/- per week; 14 and under 15, 21/- per week.

Shepherds, Byremen and Cattlemen, Pigmen and Poultrymen.

The expression week as related to these rates means a week of customary hours; for **Ploughmen** and all other Male Workers (except casual workers and milkers) it means a week of 52½ hours form 1st February to 31st October and 44 hours from 1st November to 31st January, with the addition, in the case of **Ploughmen**, of not more than 7 hours per week for stable work.

Casual Male Workers - The minimum rates proposed are : **18** and over, **10d** per hour; **17** and under **18, 8d** per hour; **14** and under **17 6d** per hour.

The proposed minimum rates for overtime employment of male workers (except casual workers and milkers) are as follows :

On Week Days **18** and over 9^1/$_2$d per hour; **14** and under **18 6d** per hour;.
On Sundays = The rate for all age groups 1/- per hour.

These overtime rates are applicable to Shepherds on any of ten days paid holidays (including New Year's Day) allowed in each year of employment; to Byremen and Cattlemen, Pigmen and Poultrymen, on any of seven days paid holidays allowed in each six months of employment; to Ploughmen and all other Male Workers (except casual workers and milkers) for all employment in excess of the hours applicable to these classes, after Non on the agreed day of the weekly half-holiday, in three days paid holidays (New Year's Day and two hiring days) allowed in each year of employment and on Sundays (except in the case of Ploughmen for hours spent on stable work within the weekly maximum of 7 hours).

Female Workers (excluding dairy and domestic workers and milkers) The proposed minimum rates are as follows:-
18 and over, 7d per hour; **15** and under **18, 6d** per hour; **14** and under **15, 4^1/$_2$d** per hour.

The proposed minimum rates for overtime employment are as follows:-
On Week Days **18** and over, 8d per hour; **15** and under 1 per hour; 1 and under **15, 6d** per hour.
On Sundays - All age groups 1/- per hour.

These overtime rates are applicable to all employment on Sundays, after Noon on the agreed day of the weekly half-holiday, on three days paid holidays (New Year's Day and two hiring days) allowed in each year of employment and to all employment per week in excess of 52^1/$_2$ hours from 1st February to 31st October and 44 hours from 1st November to 31st January.

Milkers:- The minimum rates are as follows:-

(a) House and garden, ... 3/- per week.
(b) Meals, ... 22/- per boll.
(c) Milk, ... 1/- per gallon.
(d) Potatoes, ... 75/- per ton.
(e) Coal .... 35/- per ton.
(f) Lodging in a bothy (with fire, light, furnishings,
    and attendance), ... £8 per man annum.
   Lodging in a bothy (with fire, light, furnishings,
    but without attendance), ... £8 per man annum.

(g) Board and lodging :-
    (i) Lamber boarded with shepherd, ... **£1** per week.
    (ii) All other single male workers (boarded and lodged by an employer or by another worker) :
        18 and over, ... 18/- per week.
        Under 18, ... 15/- per week.
(h) Keep of cow and followers, ... 10/- per annum.
(i) Keep of dog, ... 1/6 per dog per week.

Any objections to these proposals should be lodged with the Secretary to the Committee, Mr J. R. CLARK, York Buildings, Queen Street, Edinburgh, 2 not later than Saturday, 19th March.

Objections should be in writing and should state precisely the grounds for objection.

Copies of the full text of the Resolution may be obtained on application to the Secretary.

The Auld Crafters Roup

Auld Margret was sonsie & roond as a ba',
She'd grown unco frail & her claes werna braw,
Aye weel pleased and easy, her wark had tae bide
  Tho' lang syne the belle 'o' bonnie muir-side,
  Her man had been beadle for mony a day,
  But as last he himsel' was weel happit wi' clay,
  an noo comes her roup asn event in the muir,
  The 'effects' were as iced as hersel I am sure.

A gey puckle folk gatherd roon the hoose door,
Fin counted I thnk there was fully five score,
Some o them had cone wi intentions to buy,
  An ithers nae doot a' the ferlies tae spy,
  While I daunert doon just to do a jot wark,
  The auld auctioneer had appointed me clerk.

First cam twa or three dishes wi' hunders o' cracks,
  an auld timmer ladle, a boxie o' tacks,
  A girdle, a brander, a toaster, some mats,
  An a strong metal trap for catchin the rats,
  A dizzen tin pans, some auld knives and forks,\
  an ancient saut bucker, a baggie o' corks,\
  a cracket tea kettle withou bow or lid,\
for the haile rickmatick, just five shillings was bid.

A chissel, a cheese cloot, a wag at the wa',
  a hammer, a gimlet, a roosty bauld saw,
  A box fu' o' sundries, the staff o' a flail,
  a sma' metal pottie for makin' the kail,
  A tether, a brander, a sieve an' a riddle,
  A big mustard pot, a bit o' a fiddle,
  A three legged stule wi' the lave knockt doon,
  Tae a wyllie auld neebour at just half a croon.

A moch eaten table, a trool an' a churn,
The boords o' a bellows that had lang daen its turn,
a big easy chair wi' the back o't awa,
A roon hardwood table that stood on a claw,
A ruskie, a shovel, an' three timmer pails,
Twa bake boards, a roller and some pailin nails,
A box iron and heaters, a moose trap, a stob
the puckle fin selt, jist cam tae three bob,
I'm sure hardly ony p' them ever wad mend,
But some gaed to Pitmeakie an' some to Loaneing.

A flagon, a spaid, an' a bit o' a rake,
The silt o' a barrow, an auld herrin rake,
A green paintit tub, a cat an' six kittens,
A cradle weel worn wi' rockin' the littlins,
A few rage o' blankets, a timmer bedstead,
Twa coorse cotton sheets, an'a rough tykin bed.

A het water bottle tae keep aff the cauld,
For seven an' sixpence this lottie was sauld,
a thraw crook, a bettle, a bundle of books,
a bowster, a bird cage, a swey and three crooks,
A mild coo that wantit a gird an' a lug,
An auld spinin' jenny, a rock an' a reel,
A muckle box barrow it hadnae a wheel,
A hillock o' rubbish that cudnae be named,
By auld Jamie Muggins at sax shilllin's was claimed.

An auld muzzle loader withoot lock or stock,
A brose caup, a spurtle, the face o' a clock,
Some bits o' a chair, the frame o' a harrow,
A dizen bottles, bits o' rope, yarn and tow,
An auld flaughter spaid an' the back o' a heow,
This lot Sandy Harris wis anxious to gain,
An' for three an' a penny the trash was his ain

An auld battered rooser withoot rose or spoot,
A bress jeely pan its buddom wis oot,
A milk search, a scummer, a scythe, straik an' sned,
It couldna' weel cut fir it wantit a blade,
A hammer, a dresser some brushes an' kaims,
A besom, a scrubber an' twa winda frames,
A bucket, a door mat an' a queer stuffed canary,
Gaed for twa an' eleven to dounce Jame Carrie.

The hawkit coo crummie cam neist on the list,
Wi' nae muckle beef on her banes wis she blest,
The bidden raised slowly by florin an' croon,
'Til at four poun' ten shillings the hammer cam doon,
The shrger bit stirkie was last tae be sauld,
Its bouk wasnae big altho' thriteen week auld,
Nae sweet milk it got, sae twis jist skin and bane,
Twas selt for a poun' an' the rope was dune.

The effects o' the widow ance treasured wi' pride,
Noo ower the haill parish is spresd far an' wide,
The stob thackit hoosie by her coontit braw,
Gin it getna a tenant it shortly will fa,
Sae like dentie auld Marget we hae but oor time,
O' the treasures o' earth that tae us lok sae fine,
For some day ere lang daddy time on the wing,
Will flits frae the warld tae which oor herts cling.

The Clydesdale

Thudding hoof and flowing hair,
Style and action sweet and fair,
Bone and sinew well-defined,
Movement close, both fore and hind.

Noble eye, and handsome head,
Bold, intelligent, well-bred;
Lovely neck, and sholder laid,
See how shapely he is made.

Muscle strong, and frame well-knit,
Strength personified and fit;
Thus the Clydesdale - see him go
To the field, the stud, and show.

Proper back, and ribs well-sprung,
Sound of limb and sound of lung;
Powerful loin, and quarter iwde,
Grace and majesty allied.

Basic power - living force -
Equine King - The Clydesdale Horse.

Great Days of the Heavy Horse

The Clydesdale breed has experience several important peaks. The first, for exports, was in 1911, when no fewer than 1617 stallions and mares were exported.

The second was the demand for horses of any kind during the First World War. There was a need for more and more plough horses, as British farming boomed; but the demand for draught horses for the holocaust in France was voracious. It was, for a year or two, a case of breeding any one's son with nobody's daughter.

After the false boom in the war years, the true peak of prosperity for heavy horse breeding came in 1921. The following year, the society's membership was up to 78 life governors, 1581 life members, and 2269 annual members.

Baron of Buchlyvie.

After a distinguished career, his upper near foreleg was broken by a kick from a mare, and he was destroyed, and buried in the rose-garden at Dunure Mains. Four years later his remains were exhumed and set up on exhibition in the museum in Kelvingrove Park, Glasgow. Some people may argue that for all practical purposes the Clydesdale breed is as dead as the Baron - and few things can look more dead than a Clydesdale's skeleton.

When it comes to famous stallions, however, there will never be one to beat the Baron of Buchlyvie. James Kilpatrick of Craigie, Kilmarnock, bought him in partnership with William Dunlop of Dunure, Ayr, who later claimed he had bought out Kilpatrick. Their

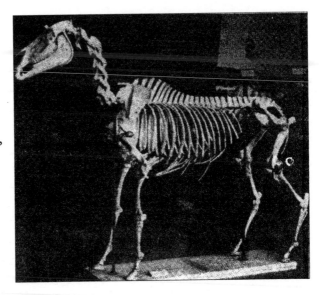

dispute over this echoed round the world, going through the courts right up to appeal in the House of Lords when the Lord Chancellor, the Earl of Halsbury, found for Kilpatrick, whose expenses were something over £6000. When the partnership was dissolved by an auction sale at Ayr in 1911, the horse was bought by Dunlop for £9500 - a world record which still stands. The two Clydesdale worthies did not speak for 22 years. Bearing in mind that the current equivalent of such a price would be around £250.00, it is hardly surprising that even the Americans thought the deal fictitious. But the stallion's earnings were as high as £3000 following the case, although 21/2 years later when kicked by a mare the Baron had to be destroyed. The skeleton is still on permanent display in Glasgow's principal museum. Dunlop later acknowledged that he had overstepped the bounds of sanity in the matter, but claimed he could not have rested without possessing the horse. If ever a stallion was exploited it was the Baron's son, Dunure Footprint, whom Dunlop named after the line in Longfellow's "Psalm of Life" - "footprints on the sands of time," so convinced was he that this was the ideal horse. He was proved right because the Ayrshire farm became the Mecca of horse-

Dunure Footprint, son of Baron of Buchlyvie, and possibly the world's most famous and prolific heavy stallion.

breeders. At the height of the season the stallion was serving a mare every two hours day and night. It took the milk of two cows, countless eggs, and heaven knows what else to sustain the effort. Terms were 60 guineas at service and 60 guineas when the mare was proved in foal, and so the financial reckoning was enormous.

Stallion fees

In later years, as the stories circulated, people began to doubt the truth of this horse's libido. But plenty of evidence supported it. One groom recalled staying at the farm and being awakened at 2 a.m. to be told it was his mare's turn - and that was at the start of the season in April, but even so she was the hundredth to visit Footprint. When Dunlop's accounts were seen later, for the year 1921, they showed stallions fees of £9690 and the horse was said to have made £15,000 in two seasons.

6 pairs on a farm somewhere in Angus

Ned Gibb

Bolshan Bothy

Jarret Brothers, Blacksmith's Chapelton, Angus

Auchrennie Farm Carnoustie 1937. from left: Grandson: W. Aitkenhead. J. Nicol,
Son: W. Aitkenhead. G. Reid. Greive: William Nicol. William Brown

The late Allan Macrae, Forebank Farm, Brchin, with Dougall dressed in his show harness

Craigie McQuaid. Stud Horse 1925

Newton of Boysack Farm Angus. (Mid thirties)

Prince & York	*Chance & Joe*	*Sharp & Jim*
(Andrew Findlay)	*(Erch Ferrier)*	*(Wull Clark)*
Clyde & Jock	*Tam & Jock*	
(Andrew Mᶜ Ewan)	*(Dod Walker)*	

Clydesdales dragging timber at Callandar

Friock Mains Farm, Angus. (1930's)

Foreman: J. Lowe   R. Smith   J. Hosie

Norman (Nor) Christie

Willie Nicol age 16 Home Farm, Kinblethmont 1926

Arrat Farm, Angus

Finally

To finalise, I have put together mostly my own experiences as a laddie and on to my later years, but never changing my opinion of the men and their manners, who, along with their dandy pair of Clydesdales, were a pleasure to watch at work.

There was very little noise - just the soil passing over the plough with the furrow as straight as if it had been drawn by pencil, also the ploughman's quiet commands to his pair. They took great pride in their lovely animals, their harness, their implements which, when added together they took part in competition, as could be seen at the ploughing match, even returning the following day to judge for themselves why someone was considered better than them.

Can you imagine? - there was a prize for the best-looking ploughman at the match. One old timer told me that was male judges' opinions, but there was a dance in the evening, and that's where the young ladies gave theirs.

And I suppose, many a heart was broken after the ball. The memories we are left with are mostly in song or a distant picture.

When the horses went off the land, the way of country life went with them. In their honour, all we can say is, "a job well done."

And Will Ye No' Come Back Again.

Acknowledgements.

The Scottish Farmer for extracts, March 1938 & April 1997.
Agricultural Wages Regulation 1937. Clydesdale Centenary.

The Herald., February 1994
"Horseman's Word" by A. C. McKerracher.